Perspective in Foreign Policy

Perspective
in Foreign Policy

By
CHARLES E. OSGOOD

Second Edition
Revised and Enlarged

PACIFIC BOOKS, *Publishers*
Palo Alto, California

Contents

PROLOGUE: PERSPECTIVE   6

Chapter 1. THE UNEASY STATUS QUO   9

Chapter 2. ESCALATION AND DE-ESCALATION
AS POLITICAL STRATEGIES   19

Chapter 3. SOME INGREDIENTS OF PERSPECTIVE   35

Chapter 4. CALCULATED DE-ESCALATION IN ASIA   58

Chapter 5. BUT WHAT DO WE DO IN VIETNAM?   71

EPILOGUE: PATIENCE   90

Prologue: Perspective

TWO PRIME FACTORS governing international relations in this century have entered into dynamic interaction during the present decade. The first is the tide of rising expectations borne on the wings of communication and transportation technology. Inequities in the status quo, between "have" and "have-not" countries and between "have" and "have-not" peoples within countries, have become the major source of energy behind national and international conflicts. The second is the development of nuclear weapon technology. Not only has the sheer capacity for destruction increased many thousand-fold, but offensive capabilities have completely outrun defensive capabilities. Our present policy of mutual deterrence vis-à-vis the Soviet Union is a natural reflection of this state of affairs. But contrary to the implications of the term, mutual deterrence is not a stable balance of power: the same fear that deters also drives an arms race, a search for ever more destructive weapons and a search for means of protection and defense.

These two factors come to a common focus in the so-called "wars of national liberation"—rebellions against foreign domination and revolutions against domestic tyranny—whether instigated from within or from outside a country's borders. Mutual nuclear deterrence tends to freeze initiatives of traditional sorts by the polar powers, and the use of nuclear weapons against non-nuclear opponents seems inappropriate, to say nothing of immoral, in conflicts of this order. This poses the fundamental problem for foreign policy in the mid-twentieth century: How can a nation like the United States use its immense power and wealth for what it defines as benevolent ends? How can it get unfrozen in this nuclear age? Unfortunately—because we have persistently defined our ends in terms of our fear of Communism—we have found ourselves on the side of the "haves" and against the "have-nots," and thus against the very tide that we have done perhaps the most to create.

The situation of the United States in Vietnam is symptomatic of a more general foreign policy disorder. The danger is that in dealing with this particular symptom we may become fixated on an essentially maladaptive, neurotic form of national behavior. Our position in Vietnam is like that of a great mastodon which has stumbled into a quagmire and in its angry struggles is sinking itself deeper and deeper. Trumpeting and flailing, we are trying to "escalate" ourselves out of the mess by military means, and in the process we are bringing death and destruction to those we presume to defend as well as to those we oppose. Yesterday we were talking about negotiated settlement as the aim of all this—but it is difficult to conceive of any negotiated settlement which could simultaneously guarantee a non-communist South Vietnam and the return home of our own military personnel. So today we are talking about "victory"—but over whom and how defined remain obscure.

However, this is now water over the dam. The Administration has been successful in creating a sense of commitment to Vietnam. Without any declaration of war, it is evident that most Americans feel that they are actually in a state of war. Where yesterday peace marchers were greeted at worst with puzzled stares and at best with tolerant grins, today they are spattered with eggs and red paint. Government spokesmen like General Maxwell D. Taylor have let it be known that such demonstrations do "give aid and comfort to the enemy," thus prolonging the war. I would say that, even if this were the case, it would be a small price to pay to preserve one of our basic freedoms, the freedom to dissent. I hope that the government will be able to extricate itself from the Vietnam quagmire, with a minimum of pain and suffering for ourselves and for others, and will then be able to turn its energies toward developing more constructive, long-term policies. For there will be more Vietnams, more Dominican Republics, more African Congos, for as far into the future as we can see. The purpose of this little book is to try to put present crises into long-term perspective, suggest some lessons we can learn from them as a nation, and offer at least the outline of a kind of policy toward the rest of the world that is appropriate to the nuclear age in which we now live.

CHAPTER 1

The Uneasy Status Quo

STATUS QUOS EXIST only to be changed. This is because, we humans being what we are, they are never equitable. Inequities in the status quo provide the driving force behind international relations. The policies of nations toward one another are essentially strategies for maintaining or changing the existing status quo in terms of self-interest. But what is perceived as "self-interest" may be blinded by short-term greed and fear or may be enlightened by long-term perspective. And the advent of the nuclear age has changed the rules; what used to be obvious in international politics is no longer so. Our leadership will succeed or fail in foreign policy to the extent that it does, or does not, achieve perspective.

Method in Madness

I assume that there must be some method behind the apparent madness in our recent foreign policy in Vietnam and elsewhere. I have known some of the men now making the decisions personally. They are not mad; they certainly are not stupid; nor are they in any sense evil. They are as dedicated to the welfare of the nation and the cause of peace as anyone reading this book.

But, being human like the rest of us, they can make mistakes. And herein lies a difference between us: Whereas it is relatively easy for you or me to admit that we have been wrong and change our ways, it is extremely difficult for leaders—particularly those elected in the democratic process. To admit making mistakes comes close to committing political suicide. To maintain political viability, mistakes may be imbedded in a larger context of decisions until they become lost to public view—this seems to be happening in the Dominican Republic. Or they may be compounded with still larger risks in the same direction, in the hope of proving that they were not mistakes at all—this seems to be happening in Vietnam. As every good poker player knows, this last is a dangerous course. One is likely to get caught up in the momentum of justifying past decisions and carried beyond the point of no return.

Just what is the method behind our recent decisions? It is, of course, impossible to capture anything so complex in a neat phrase—so I shall try to do so. President Johnson's foreign policy might be characterized as *the independent application of power to get action toward benevolent goals.* To my mind, there is no question about Johnson's benevolence: Just as he declared war on poverty within our own borders, so is he eager to declare war on the evils outside our borders—on social and economic inequalities, on ignorance and disease, and on the communist way of life. I think he would like to see us achieve a Golden Age of Prosperity, world-wide and in our own time. We have the economic and military power—more than any other nation or combination of nations on the face of the earth has ever had before— so let us wield the carrot and the stick wisely and get on with it.

Contrast this philosophy with that which seemed to characterize the Kennedy administration: *firmness and patience in the search for benevolent interdependence.* President Kennedy perceived—correctly, I think—that the only real security for any nation in a nuclear age lies in developing interdependencies with others, to such an extent that aggression becomes equivalent to suicide. Except for cancer and occasional split personalities, this also holds for the parts that make up the whole of each human individual. While practicing firmness in resisting aggression from others, as in the Cuban crisis, Kennedy preached patience; again and again he told us that the real war in men's minds, between democratic and totalitarian ways of life, would not be won with weapons, nor would it be won tomorrow or next year or even in the next generation.

Madness in Method

Why do I think there is madness in our present method? Although the application of force may often be considered "benevolent" by the men who wield the stick, it seldom is seen this way by those on the receiving end—or those who are, for the moment, mere bystanders. There is a fundamental psychological incongruity here, and it is revealed in some of our actions in Vietnam: We say that we are trying to bomb the North Vietnamese into negotiation; I say that you can bomb someone into surrender, but not into honest negotiation. We showered leaflets over North Vietnam—stating that the Chinese are their real, traditional enemy, not us— and then we followed this up within hours with a heavy bombing attack; I submit as a psychologist that there is no more certain way to convince the North Vietnamese that the Chinese are their real friends!

Failure in the application of force at one level usually leads to escalation to higher levels, particularly when the applier possesses almost unlimited power—at least, this is the lesson of history. Paradoxically, success in military escalation does not necessarily mean a successful long-term foreign policy. This strategy becomes more likely to be used in the next situation, and the next, and the next—until we find ourselves policing the world with our benevolent self-interest.

Perspective and Patience

The fundamental change in foreign policy between the Kennedy and Johnson administrations comes down, as I see it, to a narrowing of perspective and patience. This may sound rather strange—quite unlike the familiar vocabulary of foreign policy debate. But this is precisely because such elements provide the pervasive framework within which the more visible day-to-day decisions are made.

Does this change reflect differences in the personalities of these two men? Newspaper columnists frequently apply such terms as "restless," "driving," and "impulsive" to President Johnson. I have no first-hand knowledge about this. However, some of his public actions do suggest impatience: The quick decision to bomb the mainland bases of North Vietnamese gunboats when one of our naval patrols was attacked in the Tonkin Gulf (and damaged to the extent of one bullet hole, as I understand it) is a case in point. Sending U.S. Marines into the Dominican Republic without waiting for the true complexion of the revolution there to become clear is another.

I realize that there is a great deal of information, both about long-term policy and about specific situations, which is unavailable to me as an ordinary citizen. But this state of affairs in itself should be of concern in a democracy that is not, officially, in a state of war. To contribute effectively to the solution of the critical issues now facing our society— issues that certainly affect their well-being—citizens need information about ends and means, very little of which requires classification for security reasons. The students and professors who have been trying to intensify debate on the whys and wherefores of Vietnam are to be commended for their sense of responsibility as citizens rather than scorned as irresponsible upstarts.

One ingredient of perspective is understanding of our own long-term goals as a society. Another is understanding of how the advent of the nuclear age has changed the rules of the game. It may be comforting to dream about going back to the good old days, in foreign policy as well as other things, but the only way we'll do it is via a nuclear convulsion the consequences of which are literally inconceivable. The scientific knowledge which creates nuclear warheads and missiles to deliver them, to say nothing of chemical and biological weapons, exists and we can't wish it away. We have to live with it or die with it.

I think we can agree upon our long-term goals. First, we want to *survive,* with as much of happiness, health, and the other good things of life as we can muster for ourselves and those to come after us. I put this primitive value first, because without life there is very little we can do about anything else. Second, we want to *preserve our way of life*—basically, one in which the individual has relatively large degrees of freedom of choice as compared with the state which governs him. But more than this, I think we want to extend our way of life to others, not by force but by encouraging them to try it on for size and, it is hoped, to find it good. This is not to imply, by any means, that our way of life is perfect, particularly as practiced, and needs no improvement.

Status Quos

In order to understand how the nuclear age has changed the rules of the game, we must first know what the game is. If I may try to cut down to the bare bones of the matter, *the foreign policy game is concerned with maintaining or changing the status quo.* At any given moment in time, and between any pair of nations, there exists a status quo. It is the state of things as they are—not necessarily, of course, as they ought to be in terms of some ideal. As a matter of fact, given the effervescence of human minds, it is unlikely that the real status quo can ever be equitable, fair, and just for all concerned. It is out of inequities in the status quo that the dynamics of international relations spring. The status quo is more than lines or colors on a map representing spheres of influence; it is more than a balance or imbalance of military power; it includes balances or imbalances in flows of gold reserves, communications, culture, or even tourists; and, of course, the imbalance between "have" and "have-not" countries today is part of the status quo.

It may help to imagine the *real* status quo as an irregularly waving solid line between nations A and B, upon which may be superimposed a straight dashed line, representing some *ideal* status quo. This means that between two roughly balanced nations, there will be some regions where the real status quo bulges in favor of A and others where it bulges in favor of B—both being sources of conflict, but in different directions. Between an extreme "have" nation and an equally extreme "have-not" nation, the solid line may hardly overlap the dashed ideal, and all the pressure for change will be in one direction.

Not too surprisingly, it has been characteristic of "have" nations that they opt, often quite blindly, for maintaining the status quo—whatever it may be—and characteristic of "have-not" nations that they strive to change it in their favor. In today's world it is the relatively "have" nations that also have nuclear weapons; in tomorrow's world this will no longer be true, a fact that should make a lot of people do some hard thinking.

Some Paradoxes of the Nuclear Age

One of the paradoxes of this nuclear age is that the more military power a nation has, the less freedom of initiative it has for changing the status quo by use of that power. Not only does the possession of incredible power for destruction make reasonable men cautious about its misuse, but the possibility of retaliation in kind renders crass risk-taking most unattractive. The "have-not" nations do not suffer the same restraint. In a canoe, it is much more dangerous for a big man to throw his weight around than for a little one to do so.

Another paradox is that "have" nations are spending billions of dollars or rubles building weapons which they sincerely hope never to use—surely something which will be viewed as a special kind of madness in some wiser age. Even the Chinese have indicated willingness to agree to a "No-First-Use" pledge (once they have something to use). But, in this case, how do "have" nations maintain the status quo or, more wisely, try to monitor its change?

Yet another paradox of the nuclear age is that the more a nation spends in the name of "defense," the less real security its citizens have. Why? Because invulnerable nuclear weapons can only deter; they cannot defend against equally invulnerable nuclear weapons possessed by others, once they are actually used. This situation must become even more true as nuclear capabilities proliferate across the globe.

These, then, are some of the special conditions, created by our knowledge of physical science and skill in engineering, which must be kept in mind when evaluating alternative policies. It is in our long-term self-interest to follow a policy which ultimately will eliminate our need for reliance upon such nuclear defenses.

Mutual Deterrence

This is our present policy vis-à-vis the Soviet Union. Over the past two decades we have been gradually pushed into this posture from our traditional stance of "peace through military strength." In a situation where either side can expect inevitable retaliation with invulnerable nuclear weapons—retaliation which would probably eliminate half of one's own population and certainly eliminate one's own nation as a viable entity—"victory" becomes a meaningless word to all but the foolish. Note that mutual deterrence is thus a special case of interdependence between nations, forced upon us by the nuclear age—it has become suicide for one major nuclear power to attack another.

But, taking the long view of things, mutual deterrence is *not* the stable balance these words seem to imply. There are two reasons for this: Within the deterrence system, the same mutual fear which deters also serves to drive an arms race; there is thus an inherent instability which, given the advantage of surprise, encourages preventive attack (because one thinks he's far enough ahead) or pre-emptive attack (because one thinks the other thinks he's far enough ahead). Externally, the mutual deterrence system is continually coming apart at the seams because of excursions, large and small, of nations not restrained by this new kind of interdependence. Situations like that in Vietnam can escalate to full-scale nuclear war, if major nuclear powers come to see their vital interests involved. In the last analysis, the very best a policy of mutual deterrence can offer us is a world spinning toward eternity, *frozen*—armed for mutual annihilation and kept from it by nothing more than mutual fear.

The Basic Problem

How can we get *un*-frozen in this nuclear age? How can we regain the initiative in foreign policy? A great deal of thought has been devoted to this problem in recent years. There are two fundamental approaches, one stressing tension-increase and the other stressing tension-decrease. Since either approach can, in theory, be abrupt or gradual, this yields four basic policy alternatives. Although all four approaches have been tried at one time or another in human history, the abrupt alternatives are more characteristic of the pre-nuclear period, and the gradual alternatives, in their explicit formulation, at least, are more characteristic of the nuclear period. These are alternative rules of the game, alternative ways of trying to change the real status quo in the direction of a more equitable, ideal status quo—assuming, of course, that all the players believe themselves to be benevolent.

Ordinary war in ordinary times, by declaration or by surprise attack, is an abrupt increase in tension to its maximum. It usually follows a period of gradual, *but uncalculated,* escalation of threats and counter-threats, along with an arms race within the technological capabilities of the opponents. It seems safe to say that between nuclear-armed opponents like the U.S. and the U.S.S.R., there will never be a declared war. Nor will a war start with any deliberate, intentional nuclear attack. Mature nuclear powers understand the new rules of the game. If all-out nuclear war does come, it will be by accident or by escalation out of some peripheral conflict. But powers like the U.S. or the U.S.S.R. can employ nuclear weapons against non-nuclear opponents to gain quick victories. There are people in Washington clamoring for us to use our power boldly in Vietnam. We *do* have the power. Viewed in long-term perspective, however, there is no surer and quicker way to lose what we think we are fighting for—our way of life. I submit that we could not maintain Pax Americana around the world by force and long remain a true democracy.

The pure pacifist position argues that, since the arms race and the dangers to survival it engenders are based upon mutual fears, the *nobler* side must eliminate itself as a source of fear—by abrupt and complete unilateral disarmament. In the long run, by applying the painful, persistent techniques of non-violent persuasion, we could preserve our way of life. Logically, this position is sound. I do not believe the Russians, or the Chinese, would attack an unarmed population—why should they? They might try to make good Communists out of us, to be sure, but with patience and perseverance we might change them more than they change us. The trouble with this rational alternative is its complete *lack of feasibility*. I don't think such a policy has a snowball's chance in Hades of being adopted by Americans, by Russians, by Chinese, or by any other nation on the highroad of nationalism. It assumes existence of the very kind of world some other policy must create.

The basic problem facing policy-makers in the nuclear age is now clear. It is to regain the initiative in operating on existing status quos, without risking security and without misusing power. It is, if you will, for a big man to learn how to handle a canoe without capsizing it in the process. Mutual nuclear deterrence is inherently unstable and, at best, can serve only as a temporary crutch. Ordinary "war as usual" has been rendered as obsolete as the musket, although many people do not realize it. Abject surrender is possible, of course, but certainly not palatable to Americans. The remaining alternatives are graduated tension increase (escalation) and graduated tension decrease (de-escalation), or some combination of these.

In the chapters that follow we shall explore these more

subtle and complex strategies. Similar in many ways, these so-called "hard-line" and "soft-line" policies differ in one fundamental respect—how the margin for risk-taking provided by our nuclear deterrent is used. I will try to demonstrate that what is called "hard" is really soft-headed and what is called "soft" is actually very hard-headed.

CHAPTER 2

Escalation and De-escalation as Political Strategies

ALTHOUGH THE MAJOR WORLD POWERS have the military capability for waging "all-out" (albeit suicidal) war, the realities of the nuclear age have imposed restraints on them which impel them toward setting more limited political objectives. In a recent article in *Look* (April 5, 1966, p. 81), General Matthew B. Ridgway, who commanded UN forces in Korea, put the matter very straightforwardly: "Currently, a great deal of loose talk in the U.S. tends to increase the probability that our military effort will become divorced from the political objective and we will stray toward nuclear disaster. . . . These hardy folks, who, like Omar Khayyam, are ready to 'take the cash and let the credit go, nor heed the rumble of a distant drum,' would be talking sense only if our political objective were unlimited . . . and if we confessed to no national morality whatever." Both escalation strategists (the so-called "hawks") and de-escalation strategists (the so-called "doves")—to the extent that they *are* strategists—appear to agree that political objectives must be severely limited and that the steps taken to achieve them must be prudently graduated. But here agreement ends: each sees the other's strategy as leading inevitably to the surrender of legitimate political objectives.

CALCULATED ESCALATION AS A STRATEGY

In one sense, escalation as a strategy is as old as the snarl of a savage beast. It is the strategy employed by two eight-year-old boys with chips on their shoulders. Given two parties in conflict, each with certain ranges of force-levels to apply and each with certain degrees of risk he is willing to take (neither usually definitely known by the other), one party gradually increases the level of force being applied in calculated steps, hoping to reach a level at which the other party becomes unwilling to continue risking before he himself reaches his own risk ceiling. However, as an explicitly formulated policy, this is the newest arrival on the scene of alternative strategies for nations in conflict. Escalation of tensions in the build-up toward total war has, in the past, been largely uncalculated. In the modern version, the exploitation of escalation, both at the level of threats and at the level of applied military force, is intended to be for political objectives that are short of all-out victory.

The most explicit statement of this strategy is to be found in a recent book by Herman Kahn, titled *On Escalation* (Praeger, 1965). Kahn is also the author of *On Thermonuclear War* and of *Thinking About the Unthinkable*—all books which raise the hackles of men in proportion to their sense of morality. Calculated military escalation is, indeed, a Game of Chicken in which two drivers rush toward each other down the middle of a road, the first one to swerve being the Chicken. Here the Game is being played on an international scale. One reviewer of Kahn's recent book titled his review "Chicken a la Kahn"! Although this kind of foreign policy can be debated on the grounds of its morality, I shall be more concerned with its rationality—or rather, lack thereof.

Up and Down the Escalation Ladder

Kahn described a hypothetical escalation ladder having 44 rungs and spanning several "thresholds," anywhere along which, presumably, strategists can make rational decisions about either ascending further or descending. Starting with Rung 1 (an ostensible crisis), and moving up to Rung 2 (political, economic, and diplomatic gestures) and Rung 3 (solemn and formal declarations), we cross the "Don't rock the boat" threshold. This leads to Rung 4 (hardening of positions), Rung 5 (show of force), Rung 6 (significant mobilization), Rung 7 ("legal" harassment), Rung 8 (harassing acts of violence), and Rung 9 (dramatic military confrontation)—which leads to crossing the "Nuclear war is unthinkable" threshold. By Rung 22, only half-way up the ladder, we have already crossed the "No nuclear use" threshold and have reached declaration of limited nuclear war.

Although Kahn spends much time delineating the delicacies of strategy on the higher rungs of the ladder, which successively cross "Central-Sanctuary," "Central-War," and "City-Targeting" thresholds, I think he grossly overestimates the control which could be exercised at these levels—and, in any case, the most interesting and realistic problems of strategy appear at the lower levels. Rung 44, at the end of Kahn's ladder, is described as "spasm or insensate war," and the analogy with sexual orgy is noted in passing.

Since no one wants full-scale nuclear spasm, escalation *as a strategy* comes down to knowing when and how to back down and get off the ladder. Of course, it is always the opponent who is supposed to back down. Kahn alludes to the problem here: "De-escalation is even more sensitive to accurate communication and shared understandings than escalation is." But Herman Kahn was trained as a physicist, and the underlying problems here are psychological. In fact, at each rung of the ladder Kahn briefly depicts the physical situation and then goes on to explore the essentially psychological factors—fears, hopes, perceptions, expectations, motivations—which might determine decision-making.

Escalation as a strategy is described as "a competition in resolve" and "a competition in risk-taking." As in the Game of Chicken on which it is modeled, it is assumed that any two "players" will differ in the level of tension they can tolerate, both for psychological (or political) reasons and for reasons of relative military power. At each rung on the metaphorical ladder, the one initiating the escalation offers both the threat of further escalation, if further provoked, and the promise of cessation, if appeased. Whether both of these messages get through with equal clarity is debatable. Again, as in Chicken, in this calculated manipulation of tension there is a premium upon appearing irrational and implacably hostile, so that one's threats will be credible. But whether this posture encourages the opponent to wilt or incites him to go his limit is also debatable.

To play this game effectively, political strategists must be able to control the reactions of their civilian populations, in both directions—damping emotional arousal which might disturb the proper gaming spirit and suppressing public dissent which might strengthen the opponent's resolve. To guarantee the success of controlled escalation, the military strategist ideally should have available *superior force* at all conceivable levels, so that the opponent can find no level at which he can withstand the pressure and so that the escalater can make his increments as gradual as he desires. Needless to say, this feature is appealing to the military mind.

The Baited Hook

If I read the signs correctly—and, of course, I may not—then this *is* present U.S. policy in Vietnam, and we have already passed Rung 8, *harassing acts of violence,* and have moved on to Rung 9, *dramatic military confrontations.* This step is right at the "Nuclear war is unthinkable" threshold. How long can we remain at this step—particularly since it is more a jungle bog than a solid platform—before crossing the nuclear threshold?

In an article in *Fortune* (April, 1965) titled " 'Escalation' as a strategy," Kahn has this to say about Vietnam: "In this complex situation the U.S. has been attempting to use its areas of advantage to counter the special strengths of the opponents, to 'escalate' the war in a calculated way, all the time trying to make it clear that it intends to abide by certain limitations—unless further provoked. In Vietnam the U.S. is clearly a nation practicing the new dimensions of escalation, reflecting its new understanding of the reasoned and restrained, yet determined, use of limited force in a world of political challenge and nuclear danger." We have the power—no one questions that—and it appears that we have decided to use it in calculated fashion.

If the Administration has indeed adopted this policy, *then it has swallowed a baited hook.* Why baited? For years this nation has been building up incredible military power; yet, for years under the Eisenhower and Kennedy administrations, political and military leaders have been made to sit on their arms—almost literally—and this is a frustrating if not downright humiliating position. Herman Kahn has offered them a rationalization for the (calculated) use of force; indeed, he has given it a hard, glittering, scholarly legitimacy. This is the bait—what is the hook?

The hook is psychological: It may be true that, *physically,* escalators can run down as easily as up, but, *psychologically,* it is much easier to keep on going up than to stop and back down. Each step in escalation makes it more difficult to achieve the "accurate communication" and "shared understandings" Kahn himself considers necessary for de-escalation. Escalation produces the very conditions, both internally and externally, which make it harder and harder to stop moving up. Internally, particularly in a democracy, a sense of commitment is created which makes backing down come close to political suicide for leadership. Externally, escalation up to some indefinite point produces hardening, rather than softening, in the opponent's resolve—which is likely to carry the escalater far beyond the level originally intended. The analogy with sexual arousal may be disturbing, but it seems valid; as every practiced seducer knows, each threshold whose passage can be induced makes it easier to induce passage of the next. This is the hook.

Escalation in Perspective

In perspective, this strategy seems to fail on every count: It serves to augment rather than damp the likelihood of nuclear war. (One can now sense a certain callousness about the possible use of nuclear weapons—in part due to a kind of "familiarity-breeding-contempt" attributable to scenarios like those created by Herman Kahn.) It encourages "have" nations to use their power to further exploit imbalances in the status quo. It undermines democratic principles internally to the point where the means of fighting obscure the ends. To the extent that it is successful (and others repeatedly drop off the ladder because of their lesser military power), then as a nation we are learning that Might makes Right and are stripping ourselves of all pretense of benevolence. Thus, in a grimly paradoxical sense, "victory" by military escalation in Vietnam could be the worst thing that could happen to us as far as our continued survival as a democratic society is concerned.

Some will argue that this future would be the best for the world in the long run, since it would avoid nuclear holocaust —but would we not eventually come to a showdown with the Soviet Union? Others will argue that it would accomplish what a weak United Nations cannot, One World, but would this world be much different than that which Hitler's Germany might have created, had he come along twenty years later and well into the nuclear age? Yet others will argue that Pax Americana would at least be best for Americans. I think these would be Americans in name and flesh but not in spirit—they would have lost what they thought they were fighting for in the process of fighting for it.

We have here a kind of domino theory in reverse. Today we are bombing North Vietnam because it is supporting the Viet Cong rebellion in the South; tomorrow we may be bombing China because it is supporting North Vietnam; and what about the day after tomorrow? Senator Richard Russell, Chairman of the Armed Services Committee, in a press inter-

view early in our escalation (May 20, 1965), recommended
that we use nuclear weapons of any size required *now* on
Red China—to guarantee a victory in Vietnam! Quite apart
from the immorality of the Senator's recommendation and
his naïveté about what will be required for a "victory" in
Vietnam, we have here in capsule form the irrationality to
which an escalation strategy leads. Why not attack the
Soviet Union *now* and get it all over with?

CALCULATED DE-ESCALATION AS A STRATEGY

About seven years ago, at the height of tensions in the nuclear confrontation between the United States and the Soviet
Union, several proposals for the control and gradual reduction of tensions in international relations appeared. One of
these was a policy paper of mine bearing the most improba-
ble title, *Graduated and Reciprocated Initiatives in Tension-
reduction.* I soon discovered that no one, including myself,
could remember the title, even though it stated the essence
of the policy proposal clearly and succinctly. Later I discovered that the initials spelled out G-R-I-T—which was an appropriate acronym, because *grit* is exactly what its execution
requires.

Running the Escalator in Reverse

GRIT is a strategy of calculated de-escalation of international tensions. It is the application of *interpersonal* communication and learning principles to *international* relations—
where the communication is more by deeds than by words
and where what is learned is mutual understanding, trust,
and respect. The fullest development of this approach, as a
policy, has been presented in a paperback of mine called *An
Alternative to War or Surrender* (University of Illinois Press,
1962).

This strategy can be thought of as running Herman Kahn's
escalator in reverse. Steps in military escalation are *unilaterally initiated;* we do not negotiate with the North Vietnam-

ese about increasing the tempo of our bombing or moving it closer to Hanoi and the Chinese border—we just do it. But each step we take threatens the opponent into *reciprocating* with aggressive steps of his own. Steps are *graduated*—to the extent that the escalation is calculated and controlled, that risk-taking is counter-balanced by prudence, and that the political objectives are limited. But military escalation is deliberately *tension-increasing*. Now, let us reverse just one of these features—change tension-production to tension-reduction—and see what we discover as a strategy.

We would have a situation in which nation A would devise patterns of small steps, well within its limits of security, intended to reduce tensions and carefully designed so as to induce reciprocation from nation B. When reciprocation is obtained, the margin for risk-taking is widened and somewhat larger steps can be taken. The direct effect of this process is damping of the escalation in mutual tensions and lessened chances of expanded war; the psychological side-effect is increased mutual confidence and trust. Both nations are gradually learning how to behave in a nuclear age.

The Carrot and the Stick

The rules we want each opponent to learn are these: (1) if he tries to change the status quo by force, we will firmly resist and restore the status quo; (2) if he tries to change the status quo by means that reduce tensions, we will reward him by steps having similar intent; (3) if he tries to take advantage of initiatives we make in his favor, we will shift immediately to firm and punishing resistance; (4) if, on the other hand, he reciprocates to our initiative with steps of his own having similar intent, we will reward him with somewhat larger steps designed to reduce tensions. This is what I mean by *calculated* de-escalation. My colleagues in psychology would recognize this strategy as the familiar process of deliberately "shaping" behavior, here being suggested for use on an international scale. Needless to say, we have to follow the same rules if we expect others to learn them, and this is precisely what we have *not* been doing in Vietnam.

Is it possible simultaneously to maintain our national security and yet to behave in such a way as to induce reciprocation from a hostile opponent? In the book already referred to, I tried to spell out in some detail how this could be done; here I can merely state the criteria without elaboration. *To maintain security:* (a) we retain during the process our capacity to inflict unacceptable nuclear retaliation should we be attacked at that level; (b) during the process we retain capacities for conventional military resistance adjusted to the level of tension existing; (c) we graduate our tension-reducing initiatives according to the degree of reciprocation obtained from any opponent; (d) we diversify our initiatives both as to nature and as to geographic locus of application; and (e) the nature, locus, and time of announcement of our initiatives are unpredictable by the opponent. *To induce reciprocation:* (a) we persistently communicate our sincere intent to reduce and control international tensions; (b) our initiatives are publicly announced at some reasonable interval prior to their execution and identified with the general policy; (c) each announcement includes explicit invitation to reciprocation, but with form not necessarily specified; (d) announced initiatives are executed on schedule regardless of any prior commitment by the opponent to reciprocate; and (e) planned patterns of initiatives are continued over a considerable period of time, regardless of reciprocations given or even of tension-increasing events elsewhere.

It should be noted carefully that this strategy does include the "stick" as well as the "carrot." We retain a minimal but sufficient nuclear deterrent as well as appropriately graded conventional forces, so that we can effectively resist military escalations by others. But we *think* of these capabilities not simply as a deterrent but rather as a security base enabling us to take the persistent, calculated steps necessary to move toward a less dangerous world. If any opponent misinterprets our initiatives as a sign that we are "going soft," and makes an aggressive probe to test his interpretation—as the Soviets did in Cuba—then we shift promptly to the "stick"; we resist firmly, and punishingly if necessary, yet calculatedly, using precisely that level of force required to restore the status quo. As a matter of fact, such probes provide the most effective kinds of learning experience—for both sides. This was the lesson I think the Soviet Union learned from the Cuban missile crisis.

Can Escalation and De-escalation Strategies Be "Mixed"?

Just as military men speak of the best "mix" of weapon systems, in order to be prepared for all contingencies, so may political theorists think about the best "mix" of strategies to obtain objectives of foreign policy. As a matter of fact, this seems to be precisely what we have been trying to do in Vietnam. With one hand we have been escalating our military effort, both in the air and on the ground; with the other hand we have been holding out an olive branch tagged with "unconditional negotiations" and "economic aid." And we have been busily talking out of both sides of our mouths in the attempt to make this posture credible. But note, first, that our launching of air attacks on North Vietnam territory represented an attempt to change the status quo rather than restore it (clearly analogous to the Soviet attempt to implant nuclear delivery systems on Cuba); and note, second, that our attempts at de-escalation have all been in the form of words, not deeds. We are discovering the hard way that this "mix" of strategies will not work.

There is a fundamental incompatibility between escalation and de-escalation strategies. To obtain the reciprocations upon which GRIT must operate, the opponent must accept as bona fide the *intent* to reduce tensions—which is a bit difficult when bombs are raining about his head. GRIT also requires that our own government be able to take the initiative in designing and executing moves of a tension-reducing nature—which is a bit difficult in the face of charges of being "chicken." In the absence of accurate communication and shared understandings—to which, Herman Kahn points out, de-escalation is more sensitive than escalation—tension-reducing initiatives are likely to be so hedged about with conditions for home consumption that they are almost certain to be rejected. Prophecies about the intransigence of the opponent are thus fulfilled, and we find ourselves pushed still further up the escalation ladder, which still further blocks accurate communication of intent and disrupts shared understandings, except those of mutual fear and anger.

Escalation and De-escalation in Relation to Negotiation

As I was writing the first draft of this section of the book on the first day of the new year, American diplomats were flying about the world—Ambassador Harriman to Poland and Yugoslavia, Ambassador Goldberg to Rome and Paris, former White House adviser, McGeorge Bundy, to Canada —all expressing our earnest desire for a negotiated settlement. There was a lull in the air bombardment of North Vietnam—although exactly the same planes were making steady sorties along the Ho Chi Minh trail in Laos and Cambodia. I had no doubts about the earnestness of our government's desire for peace, but I had grave doubts about the success of these endeavors. I made the pessimistic prediction then that these endeavors would fail—except for creating the impression at home that, as Secretary of State Dean Rusk has repeatedly put it, *they* are the ones who do not want peace. I am sorry this prediction was borne out, but it does underscore a fact about international life: if there is one thing that is true about an escalator, it is that you can't make it go up and down at the same time.

Escalation and de-escalation thus bear an intimate relation to the process of negotiation. It seems perfectly clear that a political policy of tension escalation, calculated or otherwise, can only hamper or even render impossible successful negotiations. It creates an atmosphere of resentment and distrust in which honest dealings cannot be expected. Worse, we can hardly expect those who have been bombed into negotiating to honor any agreements reached—they have every psychological justification for subsequent defection, as the Germans displayed so clearly after World War I. Calculated de-escalation, on the other hand, is explicitly designed to create and maintain an atmosphere of mutual trust within which agreements of increasing significance become possible. There is thus an intimate facilitative relation between non-negotiated steps of a tension-reducing nature and formal negotiations; there is a fundamentally antagonistic relation between military escalation and negotiation. To talk about bombing people into a negotiated settlement is deeply irrational—into surrender, yes, but not into honest negotiation.

De-escalation vis-à-vis the Soviet Union

Is all this an idealist's pipe-dream when set against the cold facts of a harsh, real world? Not at all. We have been quietly following this kind of policy vis-à-vis the Soviet Union for nearly three years, ever since the Cuban missile crisis. We did not eliminate any of our overseas bases when Khrushchev demanded it as a bargain for Cuba, but later we denuclearized bases in both Italy and Turkey on our own initiative. Since then there have been reciprocative moves in many areas, in reducing the production of fissionable materials, in cutting back military budgets, in cultural exchanges, and so forth. Note that these have not been negotiated agreements, requiring prior commitments from both sides, but rather reciprocal initiatives, requiring only post commitment for their continuation. The Soviets have even created their own name for it—*the policy of mutual example!*

Have the predicted psychological side-effects—reduced tensions and increased mutual trust—occurred? Each reader can be his own judge as to whether or not the Russian Bogey has been cut down somewhat in size over the past three years, even though the Soviet Union remains the major threat to our security by virtue of its nuclear capability. We apparently felt enough trust to send Ambassador-at-large Averill Harriman to Moscow in a fruitless attempt to gain their mediation in a negotiated settlement in Vietnam during the summer of 1965. I would argue that the Soviet Union would not have maintained its posture of relative neutrality with respect to

Vietnam (in actions, if not in words) for so long a period had
we not been successful in modifying the harshness of our
image in their eyes. Our national image is now shifting in
the opposite direction, however.

Can a Powerful Nation Successfully Apply GRIT?

The immediate answer to this question is that it is much
easier for a powerful nation to apply GRIT than a weak
nation. Yet, interestingly enough, this is one of the strategies
of international relations that can also be applied effectively
by a small nation toward a great one. I am reminded of the
way Finland, a previously conquered country with its back
right up against the mighty Soviet Union, has been able to
preserve not only its independence but its dignity. It should
be illuminating to study in detail how relations between
Finland and the Soviet Union developed following their
military conflict.

But this strategy can be applied easier by a powerful nation. It has many bulges in the existing status quo in its favor,
and each bulge—be it in terms of military allocations or in
terms of economic allocations—represents an opportunity
for calculated steps in the right direction. Does any step
which redresses the status quo in someone else's favor necessarily mean a loss for us? Fortunately, this is not the case:
the greater the well-being and security of others, Communists included, the greater in the long run will be our own
well-being and security.

But acceptance of such a controlled tension-reducing policy as GRIT requires denial of certain assumptions we usually
make about our world. One is that our invulnerable nuclear
retaliatory capability is nothing more than a deterrent. The
fact is that the same nuclear power that deters, by virtue of
its deterrent value, also provides the possessor with a margin
of security within which to take limited risks. The deep issue
of policy today is how we use this margin for risk-taking—in
ways that narrow it or widen it.

Another assumption is that the only way to maintain credibility, that we would use our nuclear weapons if sufficiently provoked, is by presenting an image of implacable hostility toward opponents. The psychological fact is that a powerful nation like the United States can create credibility without provocation—by predictably encouraging acceptable means of changing the status quo and *equally predictably* discouraging unacceptable means. This is the proper use of the carrot and the stick.

A third assumption is that the only way to change the status quo in the direction of tension-reduction is by prior commitments on both sides, usually via negotiations. This is not necessary. We can substitute *post* commitment (via reciprocation) for prior commitment (via negotiation) as the necessary condition for continuing steps designed to control and reduce tensions between ourselves and others. We have done this successfully with the Soviet Union. GRIT enables a nation to take the initiative in changing the status quo, but without provocation and within reasonable limits of national security.

Muffed Opportunity in Cuba

If our recent relations with Russia provide an example of successful application of GRIT, then our recent relations with Cuba are an example of failure to apply it where we had a golden opportunity. By all criteria, the Cuban revolution against the dictator Batista was a popular uprising. The ordinary people were oppressed, ill-fed, ill-housed, and poorly educated; even those Americans whose interests received favored treatment from Batista found it hard to stomach his regime. Despite what he later claimed, there is no evidence that Castro himself was a Communist at that time, nor did the communist underground take an active part in the revolution until a successful conclusion was in sight. We had an opportunity to make Cuba a viable demonstration of our readiness to support popular revolutions, but we muffed it.

When Castro decided to nationalize American interests

in sugar, fruit, and oil—and (as I understand it) requested a long-term loan to repay the companies involved, either at the valuation they now claimed, if they would pay back taxes, or at the valuation used for tax purposes under Batista —our government would have none of it. Led by *Life* and *Time,* a large segment of the mass media shifted abruptly from talking about progress and promise to talking about execution and dictatorship. In just a few months, the Castro image was changed from bearded hero to bearded villain. I believe history will ultimately record that we literally drove the Cuban revolution into the arms of the Soviet Union and thence to Communism.

Be that as it may, we now have Castro parading around in our own backyard like an angry little cock. Astonishing and heretical as it may sound, I would argue that we *still* could wean Cuba away from Communism, in fact if not in name, by persistent application of the kind of calculated de-escalation embodied in GRIT. The real needs of the Cuban people are for normalcy in their relations with the rest of the Western Hemisphere, particularly the United States. In a number of speeches—within the limits of his own kind of pride and amidst bursts of belligerent oratory—Castro *has* made gestures toward rapprochement, the most recent being the arrangements for dissident Cubans to migrate to the United States. As I have argued elsewhere (*The Nation,* January 5, 1963), Castro would probably reciprocate to a carefully designed pattern of graduated moves on our part—to get agricultural machinery, medical supplies, an expanded market for his sugar, and so on. If such an endeavor failed, we might suffer a little hurt pride; if it succeeded, we might gain a much more secure and friendly hemisphere.

De-escalation in Perspective

Calculated de-escalation as a strategy serves to damp the likelihood of nuclear war. It provides a controlled means by which the inequities in the status quos between "have" and "have-not" countries can be gradually redressed. One of the important characteristics of GRIT is that it does not require a high level of mutual trust for its initiation; given a sufficient amount of self-interest on both sides, a continuing pattern of reciprocative acts of a tension-reducing nature can literally *create* mutual trust where little of it existed before, which, of course, is also the case in interpersonal relations. Calculated de-escalation creates an atmosphere within which steps toward disarmament of increasing significance can be negotiated. Most people earnestly desire a more peaceful world—although they often have only the vaguest conception of what such a world would be like. They also desire the permanent elimination of weapons of mass destruction, including nuclear arsenals. It is my firm conviction that, given the existing system of competing nation-states, only some form of calculated tension de-escalation can create the security under which a progressive sequence of negotiated agreements leading to these ends could be undertaken.

CHAPTER 3

Some Ingredients of Perspective

IN THE SEARCH for perspective on present problems, it often proves helpful to back off a bit and try to view them within a larger chunk of space and time. Viewed from a planetary system many light-years away, the events that are shaking the very fabric of our lives today are all transpiring on the thin edge of one little pebble in the sky, and they will not cause the slightest perturbation in the cosmos. But this is *too* remote. Government agencies, like the Defense and State Departments, usually try to insulate a few of their brightest minds from day-to-day affairs so that they can think hard about long-term policy; but characteristically, because they are so bright, they end up getting swept into the vortex of every passing crisis. So these agencies often assign the task of Painting the Big Picture to external, but largely government-supported, research organizations like the Hudson Institute and the Rand Corporation; with remarkable regularity, they come up with perspectives which support the present policies of their sponsors. But the task also passes into the hands of unattached and uninstructed intellectuals, who unfortunately, whether in academia or outside of it, are also usually rather remote from the nerve centers of government. Thus we find a pernicious lack of perspective in the determination of day-to-day foreign policy decisions.

In preceding chapters some of the ingredients of perspective in foreign policy have been discussed. One of these is an explicit awareness of our long-term goals as a nation—the Ship of State really does need "a star to steer her by." Most Americans have a pretty clear idea of what they are against

—Communism—but only the vaguest idea of what they are *for*. Another ingredient is understanding of the ways in which the advent of the nuclear age has changed the ground-rules for the game of international relations. Politicians and publics alike keep trying to force the new into the familiar garb of the old, but it just won't fit.

In this chapter we will consider two other important ingredients of perspective: The first—perhaps surprising in the context of foreign policy debate—is the matter of *understanding ourselves*. Only to the extent that we understand the workings of our own minds as they grapple with a complex reality can we hope to achieve rationality in making decisions. The injunction of the ancient Greek philosopher, Solon, "know thyself," has particular import in our own time. The second ingredient is being willing, and able, to *think about the really unthinkable*. What are the Really Unthinkables in foreign policy? They are the things we usually take for granted, either because they seem consistent with our basic values or because they have been repeated so often by those whom we admire. Every major advance in society, to say nothing of science, has been based on the questioning of something that was considered unquestionable.

UNDERSTANDING OURSELVES

There are certain characteristics of thinking under stress that are shared by all people simply because they are human. These characteristics, perhaps adaptive in our primitive past, apply steady pressures toward escalating inter-group conflicts. Most leaders are leaders because they are relatively immune to the effects of stress, but this is only a relative matter, and they are certainly not immune to the demands of an aroused public. We forget too easily that human civilization is a fragile thing, still in its infancy as the clock of the universe measures things. Our written history extends back only about 5,000 years; go back another hundred thousand or so and you'll find us huddled in caves for warmth and gnawing on bones. It is not surprising, then, that our ways of thinking have not kept up with our monkey facility with tools. This cultural lag—between our understanding and control of things and our understanding and control of ourselves—is the crux of our problem as a species as we enter the nuclear age.

Ego Defense

Human beings display a quite understandable tendency to avoid thinking about things that are painful, threatening, and embarrassing—particularly when these things cast doubt upon their own virtue. This process extends to those other people and entities, such as one's nation, with whom one identifies emotionally. In its extreme, such ego defense leads to symptoms like repression, hysterical blindness, and even splitting of the personality. Within the normal range, it leads to selective exposure to and avoidance of information, to rationalization of facts that impugn us, to denial of threatening aspects of reality, and to closing our minds to events that are inconsistent with a favorable image of ourselves. But these defense mechanisms do not change the real world; indeed, they serve to get us further and further out of effective contact with it.

In the long chain of transfers of information from a crisis spot like Vietnam to the mind of an individual American, these defensive mechanisms are operating on each human link to create a rosier and rosier image of operations there. It begins with information officers at the scene (who think they know what the government wants told), moves on to reporters (who think they know what their editors expect), then on to editors and rewrite men (who are sure they know what the publishers want), and finally on to the individual consumer—who selectively absorbs what makes him feel good and selectively avoids or promptly forgets what makes him feel bad. Nor is leadership immune to this process of selective exposure to information. It is a well-known fact that national leaders, past as well as present—particularly during times of stress—tend to isolate themselves from critical ideas and people and to surround themselves with supportive ideas and people. To admit that this is merely human does not mean that it makes for rational decisions.

Beginning with John Hersey's vivid reporting on the devastation of *Hiroshima* (Knopf, 1946), much information about the horrors of nuclear war has been presented to the American people. They are intellectually aware of the fact that one 10-megaton bomb dropped on New York City would wipe out many millions of human lives. They know that one Polaris submarine carries in its nuclear warheads the equivalent in destructive capacity of all of the bombs used in World War II. But they deny the reality of these things emotionally. They do not make such facts a cornerstone of their political activity. Indeed, the longer they live with such potential danger, the less concern they display about it. I have even heard it argued that, since we have had nuclear weapons around for twenty years since Hiroshima and they have not been used, the probability of their use is steadily declining. This is like saying that, since we have not had a full eclipse of the sun in Washington, D.C. for twenty years, the probability of its occurring is lessening. It all depends upon the right combination of circumstances—which in the case of eclipses is highly predictable.

A recent press release (March, 1966) by the Council of the Society for the Psychological Study of Social Issues points out that most of the American people have been closing their minds to two of the ugliest aspects of the war in Vietnam—the widespread torture of prisoners by South Vietnamese troops and our own extensive use of weapons, notably napalm but also crop-destroying sprays, that cause prolonged and indiscriminate suffering. The release notes that there is no question about the facts themselves. But just as non-Germans were more familiar with the Nazi concentration camps and gas chambers than the German people were, so non-Americans are more aware of torture and napalm in Vietnam than Americans are. Why is this so? Apart from censorship (either government or self-imposed), people find it painfully incongruous that our own humane America could be associated with such things. They search for rationalizations: "This is a new kind of war in which such atrocities on both sides are inevitable." "If you accept war, then you go out to win it any way you must." Or even the more ugly, "*they* are just primitives with yellow skins—not like us—so they don't really count." And then people simply stop thinking about it.

The point here is this: If we are going to contribute effectively to our own governing, we must maintain close contact with reality, even at the expense of some aching of the ego. Conscious awareness of the true danger of nuclear war is one of the factors inhibiting recklessness in risk-taking. The fact that key decision-makers may retain this awareness is not enough; public callousness to the danger becomes a constant weight in the scales favoring escalation over de-escalation. Conscious awareness of the inhumanity of the kind of war we are waging in Vietnam is one of the factors that could produce a change in our conduct, and thereby a change in our deteriorating world image. Public callousness to the fate of the Vietnamese as human beings makes it easier to escalate to even vaster levels of inhumanity.

The Tyranny of Words

It has always been characteristic of Man, the symbol-using animal, that he keeps trying to apply the language created in his past to the world of his present and even his future. Thus the aborigines of the New World became "Indians"— the Asians our explorers expected to encounter—and no doubt this label produced many exotic expectations. Thus were the "security" semantics of World War I applied in preparing for World War II, and the French built a completely useless Maginot Line and a false sense of security behind it. Today we are also applying "security" semantics developed in the past—"mutual defense pacts," "balance of power," "security through military superiority," and the like

—in a nuclear age that is rendering these traditional concepts practically meaningless.

There are words that we control fairly well—those rich in meaning for us—and words that control us. Discourse in this nuclear age is full of words practically devoid of meaning, at least as far as the uninitiated public is concerned. Terms like "megatons," "intercontinental ballistic missiles," and "50 million casualties" are remote from anything in ordinary experience; they lack the earthy significance of words like "bread," "blood," and "mother." When combined in slickly packaged arguments, these remote and rather awesome terms can create an illusion of understanding which is more dangerous than a simple admission of mystification. Thus they can come to control our behavior in ways that have only the slightest relation to the real world.

Take for example the phrase "stabilized mutual deterrence" as applied to the existing relationship between the two major nuclear powers. This certainly has a solid, reassuring feel to it—almost like being in a medieval suit of armor! In reality, given its foundation on the psychological sands of mutual fear and distrust, nothing could be much less stable or reassuring. In other words, the semantic implications of "stabilized mutual deterrence" simply do not fit its referent. One well-known strategist has dubbed it "the delicate balance of terror." Note that in coining this phrase our strategist was also deliberately violating our sense of semantic propriety; "terror" is certainly not something our language implies can be "delicately balanced"—and yet this is precisely the state of affairs, as the Cuban missile crisis so amply demonstrated.

At the time of this writing, there is a tough, behind-the-scenes debate going on in Washington over whether to manufacture and deploy the new ABM system (anti-ballistic missile), Nike X.* It includes the Zeus, which could intercept enemy missiles outside the earth's atmosphere, and the

* My information here is from *Science*, 1965, *150*, pp. 1696–1699).

Sprint, which has phenomenal acceleration and could intercept enemy missiles within the earth's atmosphere, at perhaps 100,000 feet (and what about fall-out?). Proponents, including a unanimous Joint Chiefs of Staff, argue that deployment of this weapon system would further deter communist aggression (by decreasing the advantage of surprise attack) and that even if it did not, it could reduce our fatalities in a full-scale exchange from about 150 to about 100 million. The reader may be wondering what on earth can be wrong with building a purely "defensive" system like this, but reality is not quite that simple. Opponents, including former White House science adviser Jerome Wiesner, argue that this would throw the arms race back into full gear, since from the Soviet point of view it would minimize the effectiveness of their deterrent on us (we could attack with the expectation of reducing the cost from retaliation)—and, furthermore, what does the difference between 150 and 100 million casualties in a country of 200 million really mean as far as survival of our society is concerned? It is interesting that, in keeping with the semantics of "deterrence," the military on both sides take it for granted that their opponent *wants* to attack and is kept from it only by a credible deterrent. Even more interesting is the fact that a recent survey indicates that *two-thirds* of the general public assume that this country already has an anti-missile defense system—after all, what is a "Defense" Department for?

Some rather remarkable things are being done with words these days. By the simple omission of any reference to North Vietnamese civilian casualties, the American public is being given the soothing image of a miraculously immaculate bombing of military installations and transport facilities. By not being given reports of casualties among South Vietnamese civilians, the public is spared the discomfort of thinking about the horror of indiscriminate death-dealing; after all, if we have trouble distinguishing friend from foe on the ground, how can we expect bombs being dropped from mile-high B-52's to do so? If you pay careful attention to your news sources, you will find that Viet Cong casualties are reported in numbers, often based grimly on "body counts," whereas ours are reported vaguely as "light," "moderate," and occasionally "heavy." Or to take a different example—by simply adding the phrase, "as was expected in Washington," to each report of another nuclear test explosion by the Chinese, the full significance of these events is neatly deflected.

The point here is that, in dealing with concepts that are inherently remote, abstract, and complex, the general public, and indeed their elected representatives in Congress, can easily be given a false sense of understanding that serves to minimize rather than enhance their voice in policy decisions. This goes deeper than ordinary "news management," about which representatives of the press have a legitimate complaint. It goes right to the heart of the democratic process itself. The truth of the matter is that in foreign affairs, as compared with domestic affairs, decisions are being made by a handful of people operating under the protective mantle of "classified information." Needless to say, military escalation creates domestic conditions in which non-official voices are even further muffled.

Projection

It has been said that "man is the measure of all things." But this is true, certainly, only to the extent that man lacks objectivity. The history of science is a history of removing the bias of the observer from influence upon what is observed. The natural human tendency is to project one's own values and beliefs upon others and assume that they are shared. At the most naïve level, we project our "natural" and "normal" view of the world onto others, and then when they call crooked what to us is obviously quite straight, deem tasty what to us is obviously distasteful, and assert to be unjust what to us is obviously just, we conclude that they are either lying or abnormal in some way. At the next, more civilized level, we recognize the relativity of others' views to their peculiar background and experience, but not our own; "forgive them for *they* know not what they do." A third level is reached with difficulty by ordinary mortals; it is where we recognize the relativity of our own values and beliefs to our own peculiar background and experience—and behave with an appropriate sense of humility. I am not asserting that there are no rights or wrongs, no goods or evils; rather, I am asserting that we must search for objective criteria, criteria that are independent of our own built-in biases.

The point here is that naïve projection provides a subtle justification for escalating aggression against others. It works this way: We know that we are peaceful in intent; projecting, we assume that the Chinese, let's say, also must know we are peaceful in intent; when they call us "imperialist warmongers" and express readiness to "beat the capitalist aggressors to their knees," knowing full well that we are peaceful in intent, we conclude that there must be something inherently evil about them—and feel less compunction about using our nuclear weapons on them. This mechanism also makes it easy for us to assume that the Vietnamese see the world as we do —as a confrontation between freedom and Communism— when in fact they see it in terms of their own experience, as a struggle for national independence from colonialism. By assuming the role of the French and projecting essentially Western dichotomies upon them, we are doing more to drive the South Vietnamese people toward a Chinese-controlled Communism than away from it.

Psycho-logic

"A foolish consistency is the hobgoblin of little minds," said Ralph Waldo Emerson. He put his finger on a characteristic of human thinking that applies to big minds as well as little, in high places as well as low. This is the tendency to reduce the complex grey shadings of the real world into absolute blacks and whites. In every human conflict this mechanism operates to transform ordinary disagreements, which are complex and multivalued, into confrontations between absolute Good and Evil.

Psycho-logic creates Bogey Men out of ordinary human adversaries. It works like this: WE see ourselves as *honest, fair, kind, friendly,* and so on through the list of favorable qualities, and, of course, in our ordinary relations with other people, we are this way. Psycho-logic dictates that THEY, being defined as our enemy and against us, must be *dishonest, unfair, cruel,* and *unfriendly*—the polar opposites of all the traits we attribute to ourselves. And to match the magnitude of their evil and justify our fear of them, THEY must also be endowed with extraordinary power. Hence the suspicion in the mind of the Birchite that Communists must lurk behind many desks in our schools, behind organizations that disagree with him, and even behind many famous doors in Washington.

It is always easier to see psycho-logic operating in others than in ourselves—for example, in the naked irrationalities that permeate the controlled Chinese mass media—and this is part of our ego defense. In every country I have visited in connection with my cross-cultural research, it has been easy to see this process working on *their* conflicts—the Indians vs. the Pakistanis, the Israeli vs. the Arabs, the Greeks vs. the Turks. It is much harder for me to see the same mechanism operating in conflicts where I am an active participant —as in some debates I have had with members of the State Department! Yet recognize this mechanism in myself I must if I am to keep my balance.

Psycho-logic has many subtle manifestations. Through the attribution of negative traits, it gradually dehumanizes the opponent to the point where the WE's *can* think about the unthinkable in the destruction of the THEM's. Every crusade or holy war has been characterized by brutalities, which were flagrantly inconsistent with the morality claimed by both sides. Like a magnet, it tends to draw all issues into parallel with its own polarity, and, relevant or not, it becomes the basis for decision. Thus the hasty decision to intervene in the Dominican Republic was based upon our fear of a Communist take-over. Exactly the same behavior becomes moral if the WE's do it but immoral if the THEY's do it. Why? Because different *motives* are attributed to US and to THEM—in keeping with psycho-logic—good motives for US and evil motives for THEM. One of our government's main justifications for escalating up to bombing North Vietnam in February of 1965 was that THEY were advising, training, and arming the Viet Cong. The undenied fact of the matter is that WE had done much more in the way of advising (with some 20,000 "advisers" in South Vietnam), training (even in bases in this country), and arming (with weapons the Viet Cong were capturing and using against us). This is an instance of a big kettle calling a little pot black!

Dissonance can be created by discrepancy between what one believes and what one perceives himself doing, and it can be resolved by changing either how one thinks or what one does. If one is *constrained* to keep on behaving in a certain way, then it is his beliefs that are likely to shift toward consistency with his behavior. This is the essence of GRIT —if opponents can be constrained by self-interest to keep on behaving "as if" they trusted each other, then they are likely to gradually modify their beliefs about each other to be consistent with their behavior. This is also, I think, the basis for deep changes in attitude and belief that can occur to men in high office. If they are forced because of their positions to keep on behaving "as if" they held certain beliefs (or else eliminate their own influence entirely by a traumatic resignation), then they are very likely to change their beliefs with very little awareness of what is happening to them. Whether it is more charitable to accuse a "dove" of becoming a "hawk" for purely political reasons, or to explain his transformation in terms of the dynamics of his own mind, I do not know.

The most important point here is this: Over the past few decades we have created in our minds a Communist Bogey and have endowed it with irrational properties that obscure its true nature and render us senseless and ineffective in combating it. We see it as *monolithic* (it is not, as the deep rift between the Soviet and Chinese versions clearly shows); we see it as *unmodifiable* (it is not, as the significant changes in Russia and, indeed, as our granting of "favored country" status to Jugoslavia and Poland testifies); we see it as *implacably hostile* (it is not, as the definite warming of relations with the Soviet Union over the past three years indicates).

We have gotten ourselves into the posture of reacting blindly and violently, like a maddened bull, to one and only one property of any situation—the color of red. As Professors Don and Arthur Larson put it in a recent book titled *Vietnam and Beyond,* "Our present policy is one of 'massive containment,' in which we guarantee, at all costs, including as much military action as necessary, and at all points in the world—friendly, unfriendly, valuable, worthless, tenable, untenable—that communism shall not expand one inch." Communism is an alien and unacceptable way of life, and we are justified in fighting it; but we should be fighting against the real thing, intelligently, not against a phantom created in part by the workings of our own minds.

Fixation

Each situation in the real world of international relations, be it Suez, the Congo, the Dominican Republic, or Vietnam, is like a choice point in a very complicated maze. Policy determines which path we take. The basic policy alternatives discussed earlier are not static and equi-probable. Since nations, like individuals, learn from experience and are modified by it, the availabilities of policy alternatives keep shifting with what we do and the consequences. We learned a lesson from the Cuban missile crisis—the wrong one, unfortunately —that "when Good Guys get tough, Bad Guys back down." That situation erupted in our own backyard, but we are now trying to apply the lesson we learned in another power's backyard. If the strategy of escalation in Vietnam is successful, even in short-run military terms, we will become even more fixated upon this alternative and more readily apply it elsewhere.

This principle of fixation by experience applies to all nations. Russia, for example, has experienced a long history of invasions by land, including most recently invasions by Napoleon, by Hitler, and an abortive encroachment against the Communist revolution after World War I by the Allies, including American troops. It is a fact that, in the development of the deterrent relation between the U.S. and the U.S.S.R., the Russians have been much more concerned about land-based nuclear weapons in Europe than about the more elusive but equally deadly sea-based, Polaris-type nuclear weapons. I take this blindness on the part of the Soviets as an example of fixation by experience.

Another instance would be the fixation of the Communist Chinese upon massive land forces as an adequate safeguard against destruction in a nuclear age. Nothing could be more nonsensical. We could wipe mainland China clean of life today with our nuclear weapons and their fall-out—which is not to say that we should. Undoubtedly, as the Chinese mature as a nuclear power, as they observe and interpret the effects of their own tests, they will change their views and realize that relative masses of human bodies mean absolutely nothing in any nuclear war. But to the extent that they believe this now, they will contribute to our further escalation in Vietnam.

There is a very well-known psychological principle that operates upon choices among alternatives in decision-making: beyond some optimal level of tension (optimum for flexibility and creativity), further increases produce *stereotopy* or rigidity—in how we perceive situations and how we react to them. In effect, the most probable alternatives as determined by past experience become even more so, and the availability of other options becomes less. Paradoxically, this means that in crisis situations, when we most need flexibility and insight, we are rendered least capable of employing them. Having adopted and followed a strategy of escalation at lower levels of tension, this means that as higher levels of tension develop, we become progressively less and less capable of changing this strategy. Psychologically, we can become glued to the escalator.

THINKING ABOUT THE REALLY UNTHINKABLE

It is precisely those things we take for granted which serve to put us in straitjackets as far as flexibility in foreign policy is concerned. Thinking about hundreds of millions of human deaths in a counter-city nuclear war is "unthinkable" because it is horrifying; Herman Kahn in his book, *Thinking About the Unthinkable,* has tried to make people face this horror. Questioning "taken-for-granteds" about foreign policy is "unthinkable" because it shakes the very foundations of our world view; I ask that we face certain questions with an open mind, in the interest of gaining perspective.

Just What Is Our Responsibility to the Free World?

It is remarkable how, in the short space of three decades, we have swung a full 180 degrees from the assumption of no responsibility for anyone to the assumption of complete responsibility for everyone. Unfortunately, we define the Free World negatively, as anything non-communist, rather than positively in terms of democratic ideals. Following the dictates of psycho-logic, we have rotated our sense of responsibility into parallel with our fear of Communism.

Thus, we did not intervene militarily in the Dominican Republic when, in 1963, a right-wing and expressly anti-communist military junta overthrew the first democratically elected president, Juan Bosch, and rescinded the new constitution. Yet we did intervene in favor of the junta when, in 1965, rebels attempted to restore Bosch and the constitution. The justification given for the precipitous unilateral action, which placed over 20,000 American troops on Dominican soil within a few days, was the threat of a communist take-over. It has since been proven that this revolution was neither communist-led nor communist-inspired. Under pressure of facts and public opinion, both within the U.S. and around the world, we are now (as of this writing) trying to shift from unilateral to hemispheric action under the aegis of a somewhat reluctant OAS. It is hoped that this tiny country will be enabled to determine its own political fate—and, further, that we will have learned something significant about the nature of our responsibility in the world.

The question of self-determination is also critical in South Vietnam. Professors across the country, some of them experts on Southeast Asia, have been debating the Administration's position, primarily on the ground that the conflict there was not an invasion from the communist North but rather a civil war, with the North Vietnamese supporting one factor and the U.S. supporting the other. They point to the fact that the Viet Cong rebellion began in the South, far from the border, soon after our failure to hold the free elections guaranteed by the 1954 Geneva agreement, and the fact that the Viet Cong guerrillas have been nearly 100 per cent South Vietnamese using, for the most part, captured American weapons.

Does a shift to "red" anywhere on the map necessarily mean a relative increase in the power of world Communism? To ask this question certainly sounds like heresy, but let us consider it anyhow. In the first place, power and security *in a nuclear age* have very little to do with either geographical area or population—wealth, industrial potential, and technological sophistication are much more important. Second, expansion by a major communist power may actually have negative effects. It may create a drain on limited resources, as the Soviet Union is discovering in its attempt to make Cuba a "show-place for Communism in the Western Hemisphere." It may produce ideological factions—as the spectrum running from the deep red of China to the pale yellow of Jugoslavia demonstrates.

What is our responsibility? I believe it is to provide a consistent model of a good way of life and steady support for those who want it. People cannot be coerced or bought into a democratic way of life; it is something which must be learned by good example and by long practice. There is a fine line between support and domination, however, and it must be carefully drawn. The Marshall Plan for a devastated and demoralized Europe after World War II is an example of economic aid which effectively prevented the spread of Communism—by creating internal conditions which made this political alternative intolerable. We should worry more about supporting countries like India in ways that make them internally resistant to Communism and worry less about places where democracy has neither a tradition nor the necessary economic underpinning. In other words, our commitment to the Free World should be defined positively, in terms of the strengthening of democratic institutions, rather than negatively, in terms of the containment of Communism.

What Changes in the Status Quo Deserve Our Support?

A scant 200 years ago, our nation had its birth in a revolution against the status quo of British Colonialism. Both our position as a "have" country and our overwhelming fear of Communism have led us to forget our own heritage and assume the stance of almost blind resistance to change. Inequitable status quos exist all over the world today, both between countries and between groups of people within countries. As I indicated earlier, such inequities are the primary source of political dynamics, national as well as international, and, needless to say, Communism feeds on the energies released. Inequities between colonizing and colonized countries feed rebellions—like that of the Vietnamese against the French. Inequities between "have" aristocracies and "have not" peasants feed revolutions against the dictatorships which usually exist under such conditions—like the revolution of the Dominicans against the dictatorship of Trujillo. The problem for us is how to deal with these legitimate political energies.

On Sunday evening, May 9, 1965, in explaining our intervention in the Dominican Republic, President Johnson proclaimed the most far-reaching extension of the Monroe Doctrine since the days of Teddy Roosevelt. He declared that "revolution in any country is a matter for the country [itself] to deal with . . . [but] it becomes a matter for hemispheric action . . . when the object is the establishment of a Communist dictatorship." Aside from the fact that evidence for communist control was not then, and has never been, established, it was unilateral U.S. action, not hemispheric action, which had been taken.

There are many in Washington and elsewhere who argue that this revolution against the military junta *would have been* taken over eventually by the Communists—using the analogy with Cuba—and that therefore prompt preventive action was necessary. This argument is more than specious; it sets a dangerous precedent. Coupled with President Johnson's extension of the Monroe Doctrine, it writes a blank check for the U.S. to intervene against attempted changes in the status quo in this hemisphere anywhere and any time. How, indeed, would we ever recognize a genuinely popular and justified revolution—with the existing government crying Communist Wolf? Given the gulf between aristocracies and peasantries throughout Latin America, and the way Communism thrives on such inequities, it will be difficult to find a completely sanitized revolution.

There is no reason why the Communists should always profit from inequities in the status quo. If we accept the legitimacy of attempts to redress unjust existing conditions, then the real issue becomes the *means* by which the attempt is made.

First, we must realize that there are situations in which rebellion against foreign domination or revolution against domestic tyranny are the only means a people may have left. It is our business to keep informed about existing conditions in such countries and be prepared to support principles rather than governments, just because they happen to be anti-communist.

Second, we must seek to clarify and get codified means of external influence of one country on another which are acceptable and means which are not. Certainly the people who do the rebelling or revolting must be indigenous, even though the ideas and materials need not. I realize that the U.N. has devoted a great deal of attention to this problem, but it needs to be made a focal issue—since this is what it is. Perhaps one of the unanticipated benefits of a political settlement in Vietnam will be a new readiness on the part of China, as well as Russia, the U.S., and other major powers, to sit down to serious discussion of the rules of conflict below the level of armed intervention. We also want to exert influence on developing countries, but we should insist upon rules for such conduct and abide by them ourselves.

Am I recommending "subversion" in the support of our way of life? Of course I am. As a form of political relationship between individuals and their governments, our democratic system is far more revolutionary on this planet than is Communism. In a most insightful paper, titled "The Subversive West" (*Bulletin of the Atomic Scientists*, May, 1965), historian Theodore von Laue has this to say: "We are the beneficiaries of western civilization; therefore we are its accomplices as well. We are the cause of the chaos resulting from the triumphant subversion of all native order; we are morally responsible for all the desperate efforts to rebuild native society after the western pattern." Laue includes Russian and Chinese versions of Communism among attempts to imitate the western model, and he goes on to say: "That Great Society of ours (even with all its imperfections) profoundly humiliates all others who, no matter how hard they try, cannot match it." And, of course, the secrecy, the Berlin (and other) walls, the Iron and Bamboo Curtains, are symptoms of this sense of inferiority. We are subversive, all right, but the trouble is that we haven't gone far enough. We need to strive even harder to create those conditions which support our way of life where it already exists in approximation, and encourage it where it does not.

It is high time we appreciated the fact that we are a revolutionary society still and made it a cornerstone of our long-term foreign policy. Rather than glorifying "stability" and "containment," we should accept instability and change as necessary and natural facts of life. A final history of our time—if there is one—will probably draw its theme as being the period of intense conflict between "haves" and "have-nots," both within and between nations. There is much that we can do to transform the massive energies created by inequities in status quo into *guided and controlled change.* The wealth and the science and the sheer human energy that is now being poured into weapons—which we hope never to use—could do much to speed the world through this transition. What emerges will not be the American Way of Life as it is practiced today; it will have been transformed in the process into something that could be a much better way of life.

Are National Sovereignty and International Security Compatible Values?

When what we define as our vital interests are concerned, we insist upon our right to act unilaterally and without regard for international sanction. Both the intervention in the Dominican Republic and the escalation up to bombing targets in North Vietnam territory were in flagrant disregard of the U.N. Charter. Yet we condemned the Soviet Union (in Hungary), the British (in Suez), the French (in Algeria), and the Dutch (in Indonesia) for doing essentially the same kind of thing. We can't have it both ways. We can't expect other nations to act *inter*-dependently through international organizations if we, the most powerful nation on earth, act *in*-dependently whenever the spirit moves us.

Let us look objectively at the question of national sovereignty for a moment. Most people think—quite naïvely—that we surrender it by getting tied down by international organizations like the U.N. and the World Court, losing our freedom of action thereby, and becoming subject to the will of foreigners. There are more dangerous ways of losing our national sovereignty than by transforming it into international sovereignty. Every time we make an international commitment—whether it be to defend a Berlin or to support the regime of some avowed anti-communist general in a Vietnam —we are surrendering our sovereignty. Why? Because the only meaningful definition of national sovereignty is freedom for decision, independent of the wishes or actions of others. If the actions of Chiang Kai-shek on Formosa could commit us to a disastrous land war in China, then it would be rather ridiculous to talk about our "sovereignty" in the matter.

In this sense, this nation never has had, never could have, and never should have absolute sovereignty. Indeed, we never would have become a *United* States under a federal government had this attitude prevailed during the crucial years following the Revolution. But our proliferation of commitments around the globe amounts to surrender of our sovereignty *piecemeal* rather than by rational, orderly design. The central issue is this: in this nuclear age, every step we take in the direction of reducing our own sovereignty should be matched with equivalent steps by all other nations. This means, for one thing, that membership in supranational organizations like the U.N. must become mandatory and universal. It means, for another thing, that nations must gradually assume a relation to the supranational organization analogous to that of the states of this Union to its federal government—which in turn means a gradual differentiation of the spheres of national (state) and international (federal) authority. In a nuclear age we cannot simultaneously attain international security and retain national sovereignty in the traditional sense. And finally, of course, this means that Communist China must be brought fully into the world community.

Can We Co-exist with Communist China?

In our *official* eyes, a long-established government representing one-fourth of the people on the face of the earth simply doesn't exist. Of course, *unofficially* it exists, all right, and, in fact, continuing *sub rosa* conversations in Poland have been going on for a long time. However, the assumption that we can somehow handle issues in Asia without dealing formally with the major power on that continent is sheer nonsense (and I have found this opinion shared—privately, that is, not publicly—by almost everyone in Washington with whom I have talked). The simple truth of the matter is that we cannot stabilize *any* situation in Asia, South Vietnam or elsewhere, without working out a rapprochement with China. This in no way requires, or even implies, that we approve her form of government.

Today we see China through what Felix Greene, in the title of a recent book, calls *A Curtain of Ignorance* (Doubleday, 1964). Greene is a British lecturer and author of numerous books on international affairs. He has made several visits to mainland China. He states that "deeply implanted in the minds of Americans is the belief, the certainty almost, that of all the nations of the world today, China is the most belligerent." He draws a line between the jargon of the Chinese press and her behavior as a nation: China has not expanded aggressively in areas (e.g., Nepal) and at times when it was possible to do so. China has not contributed weapons in any quantity to other communist groups in Asia (most coming from Russia and its European satellites). The Communism of North Vietnam did not represent a Chinese take-over. The reported invasion of Laos by China in 1959 proved to be no invasion at all. And so on.

Felix Greene's book is heavily documented: with first-hand reports of others as well as himself (about actual living conditions in China today); with reports of Congressional hearings (for example, General Maxwell D. Taylor's testimony on whether, in fact, India started the border clash in October, 1962); with formal exchanges between governments (for example, John Foster Dulles' handling of China's invitation to admit 16 American correspondents on 60-day unrestricted visas in 1956). The most fateful decisions of our time hang on the understanding—or ignorance—of our people and their elected representatives about China. If North Vietnamese troops move into South Vietnam in large numbers and with moral and military support from the Chinese, and then if Chinese troops begin to move into direct and massive confrontation with American troops, we will have escalated fully onto Rung 9 of Herman Kahn's ladder, and the pressure toward crossing his "Nuclear war is unthinkable" threshold will become unbearable. Crossing it might well mean the beginning of World War III—holocaust.

I do not claim to be an expert on Communist China myself. As a matter of fact, it is extraordinarily difficult for any American to become an expert on China under present conditions of communication between our countries, or rather, lack thereof. Yet the issue of China's belligerency and expansionism must be opened to public debate. Our relation with this nation has now become the crux of our foreign policy. As I write here now (March 25, 1966), the Senate Foreign Relations Committee, under the leadership of Senator J. William Fulbright, has opened hearings on our policy toward China, and earlier Senator Robert Kennedy had urged that China be invited to participate in negotiations on control of the spread of nuclear weapons. (It is perfectly obvious to anyone but an ostrich that nuclear "have" nations are not going to restrain, and nuclear "have-not" nations are not going to refrain, as long as one major nuclear power remains outside the system of international sanctions.) Both of these senators, and other members of Congress who are joining their demand for public debate, are to be commended for their courage and statesmanship. What is perhaps most significant to note is that the opening of this debate has *not* been accompanied by the cries of outrage which many people expected. Sacred Cows, I suspect, have a way of becoming Tired Old Paper Cows, and a good, healthy "poof" will blow them into smithereens. But someone has to have the courage to go "poof."

But the problem of what we *do* about our relations with China remains. We face some pretty grim alternatives here. Imagine that we have an immature Tiger in a flimsy bamboo cage: (1) We can persist with implacable hostility, prodding and resisting counter-prodding until that point in the not-too-distant future when a full-grown Tiger bursts from its flimsy cage, armed to the teeth with nuclear weapons—and *then* decide what we can do under traumatic crisis conditions. (2) We can try to maim or even exterminate the Tiger *now*, while it is immature and we are clearly stronger. This would mean launching a preventive nuclear war, designed to eliminate China as a potential nuclear power, and then trying to live with the after-effects, both internal and external, of assuming the role of world policeman and perhaps exterminating millions of helpless people in the process. (3) We can begin *now* the long, patient process of shaping the Tiger—changing its image of us, rewarding it for acceptable behaviors, making it more and more dependent upon others—so that when it does break out of its bamboo cage, it will come forth purring rather than roaring.

Does this last strike you as pure fantasy? In the next chapter I shall try to spell out in some detail how a strategy of calculated de-escalation could be applied to our relations with Communist China. The course would not be easy, but it is beset by obstacles as much of our own making as by any innate evil of the Chinese people or leaders. To shift our foreign policy in such a direction will require both perspective and patience, including understanding of the workings of our own minds and willingness to think about the kinds of Unthinkables we have considered here.

CHAPTER 4

Calculated De-escalation in Asia

VIETNAM IS a symptom of a more general foreign policy disorder, and this disorder now has its focus in our relations with Communist China. We are not going to stabilize any situation in Asia, Vietnam or elsewhere, without reaching some rapprochement, some basis for peaceful co-existence, with this Giant of the East. China has been rapidly revitalizing itself and transforming itself into a modern industrial society, despite its relative isolation from the rest of the world and even despite the withdrawal of Soviet technological assistance during 1960. The recent setbacks China has experienced in foreign policy (for example, in Indonesia) are not going to pacify her; indeed, a redoubled surge of effort is the most likely effect internally.

I have already indicated the grim alternatives we face in our relations with China: maintaining our present stance of implacable hostility until, in the near future, she bursts loose with a full-scale nuclear arsenal; waging preventive war now, while we are clearly superior militarily, and then living with the consequences; or undertaking now the slow and patient process of restoring normal relations. In this chapter I shall describe a feasible, if difficult, course we could take toward restoring normal relations with China.

SETTING OF THE PROBLEM

This is not the place to trace in any detail the painful history whereby, in the space of two short decades, the United States has changed from the closest Western friend of the Chinese to their Personalized Devil. But at least a brief review is in order to provide a framework. In 1949, when the Communists had driven Chiang Kai-shek to refuge on Taiwan, the United States appeared willing to establish relations with the mainland government once it had demonstrated its stability—even though we had supported the Nationalists. But the Korean War changed all this: John Foster Dulles' policy of "containment of Communism" (then perceived as directed from Moscow) was extended to Asia, the Seventh Fleet patrolled the straits of Taiwan, and military and economic aid was poured into Taiwan in massive doses.

Whether Communist China's entry into the Korean War as the U.S. forces approached the Yalu is to be considered "unprovoked aggression" or not depends upon one's perspective. We might ask ourselves how we would respond to Chinese troops pushing toward the Rio Grande in Mexico; I think our response in the Cuban missile crisis gives the answer. Since that time, our policies can be viewed as an unswerving attempt to isolate China and frustrate her national goals, legitimate as well as illegitimate. Lobbying pressures by the Committee of Two Million, representing Nationalist Chinese interest and fronted by the charmingly antiquated Madame Chiang Kai-shek, as well as the persecutions of the late Senator Joe McCarthy, served to stifle dissent and mold a monolithic public opinion here at home.

Needless to say, our commitment to Chiang Kai-shek's dictatorial Nationalist regime on Taiwan as the "legitimate government of all China"—with its roughly two million refugee Chinese and ten million Taiwanese, compared with some 800,000,000 mainland Chinese under the communist system—makes it difficult to develop a rational long-term policy toward Asia. It is just a bit like trying to lead a dog by a collar around its tail. More than this, we are hamstrung by the military escalation already undertaken in Vietnam and which is now moving even further upward. Any attempt on our part to destroy the government of North Vietnam and substitute one politically hostile to China would certainly bring her directly into the war; this much we should have learned from Korea. Nevertheless, working within even these severe restrictions, it is possible to suggest at least the beginnings of a more rational policy in Asia.

DISPLACEMENT OF INITIATIVES

We have gotten ourselves into such a position vis-à-vis North Vietnam and Communist China that any direct application of a strategy of calculated de-escalation would be most difficult. Escalation and de-escalation strategies simply do not mix—and I sincerely hope our government is learning this lesson. A country that is itself being bombed, or whose immediate borders are being bombed, is not likely to view as bona fide gestures of a tension-reducing nature suddenly proffered by the attacker. Nor is our home population likely to view such gestures as anything other than evidence for "lack of resolve" once it has become committed to a military solution by its government and generally aroused by the loss of loved ones. A direct invitation by the U.S. government at this point to establish normal diplomatic relations with China would certainly be rebuffed, producing "I-told-you-so's" on all sides.

But the strategy of graduated and reciprocated initiatives in tension-reduction (GRIT) can be applied *indirectly*. It can be displaced—onto third parties, into non-critical geographical areas, and toward the periphery of the focal conflict. This is because international tension has at least something in common with money in the bank—it can be increased by deposits from many sources and it can be decreased by withdrawals to many receivers. Let us explore some of the possibilities in these directions.

Displacement Onto Third Parties

Communist China now maintains diplomatic relations with more than fifty countries; these include such mutual friends and neutrals as Denmark, France, India, Israel, The

Netherlands, and Sweden, to say nothing of the Soviet Union. France's de Gaulle has already taken the initiative in efforts to bring China back into the world community; we should quietly encourage such initiatives rather than marking France down still lower on our list of neighbors. Although neither Canada nor Japan maintain full diplomatic relations with China—for reasons that are fairly obvious—they have been enlarging their economic and social intercourse with her and are clearly chafing at the bit to open still further the Chinese market. We should quietly encourage rather than oppose this increased involvement of China with the world, because our long-term security increases as the interdependence of China with the rest of the world increases. In the broadest sense, this is an effective deterrent against aggression. If China should face another famine or flood, we should first supply aid via the intermediation of other nations, but then openly offer our own aid.

Displacement into Non-crisis Geographical Areas

It is obviously *possible* to maintain firm military resistance against an opponent in one place on the globe while steadily applying calculated de-escalation pressures in other places on the globe. But nations tend to be inflexibly monolithic in such matters. Hostility against one opponent tends to generalize to other opponents—another manifestation of psycho-logic, the consistency which is the "hobgoblin of little minds." Yet precisely such strategic flexibility—ability to apply firmness in one place and de-escalation of tensions in another, and that *simultaneously*—is a necessary ingredient of long-term policy in a nuclear age. Given the speed of international communication these days, the de-escalation in one region can help to modify our national image in another, and thereby render more credible our attempts to ease tensions at the focus of hostility and conflict.

In the last chapter I suggested Cuba as one spot where we face hostility but not open conflict and where, given the needs of the Cuban people, the calculated application of

GRIT would be quite feasible. Indonesia is another such spot where tension-reducing steps could be applied. Cambodia provides us with yet another opportunity, and there are many other places. Success in such a course in Cuba, for example, would do more than remove a thorn from our side; it would provide an example of how a great nation can resolve difficulties with a small nation without resort to force, or even threats of force, and without either nation losing its dignity. And more, this would become part of our image across the world, penetrating even into Asia. Being inconsistent with our present image of aggressive hostility in the minds of many Asians, including the Chinese, it would apply pressure toward modifying this image. I am sure that Asian minds are as susceptible to the pressures of psycho-logic as are Western minds.

Displacement Toward the Periphery of the Focal Conflict

The further one gets from the focus of a conflict, even while remaining in the geographical region of it, the easier it becomes to apply de-escalating moves. For example, if we really do not wish to bring China into the Vietnam war, we should gradually draw the radius of our bombing back from the Chinese border toward the direct access routes to South Vietnam—and keep it there. Our own military now admits that conventional air attack on North Vietnam, while obviously a hindrance and source of harassment, is not going to bring them to the negotiation table or to knock out their support of the Viet Cong.

Unilateral guarantees to observe the codes for humane treatment of prisoners (with request for reciprocation in kind), unilateral releasing of small batches of North Vietnamese prisoners (with request for reciprocation in kind), and offers to help rebuild bridges and other non-military structures once peace has been achieved (which obviously could not be reciprocated), would also inject elements of tension-reduction into the conflict situation. Giving evidence that we are aware of, and respect, the cultural traditions of others would also help our image in Asia. For example, James Reston reports (January 25, 1966) that "the people in the South Vietnam villages seem to resent the bombing of their dead more than the bombing of the living." We should explicitly take such cultural facts into account in determining our conduct of the war—strange as it may seem to mark cemeteries and avoid striking them—rather than writing these facts off as evidence for the "primitiveness" of another people. Whether the use of napalm is more or less "primitive" is certainly debatable.

DIRECT, LOW-RISK INITIATIVES

It is part of the over-all strategy of GRIT that steps taken in the early phases of its application are low in risk to our real security, are usually non-military in nature, but are high in both visibility and psychological impact. However, when mutual hostility is as high as it is now between China and the U.S., even such low-risk gestures are liable to misinterpretation and consequent boomerang effects. For example, the State Department in late December of 1965 announced that medical and similar professionals would be free to visit China; the immediate Chinese response was negative, which should not have been unexpected. For this reason, the U.S. should keep applying a steady pressure of displaced initiatives—as described above—until some signs of readiness for reciprocation appear. (And, needless to say, such pressure must not be accompanied by further military escalation of the focal conflict, although continued firm resistance is compatible.) When and if the atmosphere of hostility modifies sufficiently, direct initiatives like the following could be undertaken.

(1) *Announced willingness to accept accredited newspapermen and scholars from China and request for reciprocation in kind.* One of the results of the development of extreme mutual hostility has been the virtual cut-off of communication—the Bamboo Curtain, it has been called. In the present situation, it is almost certain that the images people

on both sides have of each other are grossly over-drawn, and therefore an increased flow of accurate information can hardly have anything other than a corrective effect.

(2) *Announced willingness to send scientists and technicians as requested by China* (with a few obvious restrictions) *and request for reciprocation in kind.* "The withdrawal of Russian advisers in 1960 from the mainland, the exacerbation of the Sino-Soviet dispute, and the disappointments of the 'Great Leap Forward' have placed Communist China in a position where it has been denied credits, developmental assistance, and advice essential to its plans for industrialization and modernization." * There is no question about the needs of China for technical assistance, just as there is no question about her resistance to accepting it after two decades of isolation. Nevertheless, the need is there and it constitutes one of the major levers we can exert upon China to induce her to reciprocate to appropriately designed initiatives. Furthermore, we would be wise to look actively for those aspects of *Chinese* science and technology from which *we* can profit; this would help reduce resistance due to pride.

(3) *Announced termination of our total trade embargo with China and encouragement of trade between U.S. and China in non-strategic materials.* This, by the nature of things, must be a purely unilateral action without request for reciprocation. At present, any American tourist who (often unknowingly) buys some item "Made in China" (the wrong China!) finds it stripped from his possession by U.S. Customs upon his return—and without remuneration. This is a petty business in the relations between one great nation and another with whom it is not actively at war, and it obviously does nothing to improve them. Although it is likely that the flow of trade would be somewhat one-sided in its early phases, it is equally likely that this would not remain true for long.

* From *A New China Policy: Some Quaker Proposals,* a report prepared for the American Friends Service Committee, 1965. This is an extremely insightful and well-balanced presentation of the past, present, and future in our relations with Communist China.

The fundamental thing is to create an expanding network of *inter-dependencies* between Communist China and the rest of the world, including the United States, thereby increasing her awareness of the real cost of disrupting these sources of gratification.

(4) *Announcement of readiness to receive both tourists and immigrants from mainland China and request for reciprocation.* The free flow of tourists in both directions provides corrective information about the ordinary lives and concerns of people on both sides. The more permanent exchange of people as immigrants can provide (although it does not necessarily do so) an inhibition against mutual national aggression. In this connection, it should be mentioned that prior to the abrupt freeze in our relations in 1950, Americans and Chinese appeared to find personal relations relatively easy and warm, probably because of considerable congruence in interpersonal norms; this has continued to be true of relations with immigrants from Nationalist China. Again, given the present inequities in economic status quos and population pressures, it is likely that these flows of persons would be lopsided in the beginning, tourism greater from the U.S. to China and immigration greater from China to the U.S., but, also again, these flows should gradually tend to balance out.

It is important to stress that none of the direct initiatives suggested in this section, or in the previous one on displaced initiatives, threaten our real security. Indeed, they are designed to ward off the extreme threat that would be posed by a nuclearly armed and still implacably hostile China in the near future. It is also important to note that there is no necessary correlation between the military significance of tension-reducing initiatives and their psychological impact—as the first Sputnik made eminently clear. It should also be noted that none of these moves implies approval of the form of government of Communist China; we maintain reasonably normal relations with Fascist Spain (and many other dictatorships around the world) as well as with the Soviet Union (and many other communist governments), without in any way approving of their forms of government. This is the essence of the notion of "peaceful co-existence."

The real resistance to calculated de-escalation of the sort I have described here comes from the primitive reasoning that "What is *good* for THEM must be *bad* for US"—which will be recognized as pure psycho-logic or emotive thinking. The truth is that what is good for THEM, in health, economic well-being, education, and security from external threat, is also good for US in the long run.

COMMUNIST CHINA AND THE U.N.

If it weren't so deadly serious, one might describe the U.S. posture with respect to China and the U.N. as ludicrous. We have nothing to lose and everything to gain by having Communist China represented in the U.N.—and, indeed, at the level of a permanent member of the Security Council—to engage her in debate on fundamental issues, to involve her in the deliberations of such U.N. bodies as the International Atomic Energy Commission, the Population Commission, and the Economic Commission for Asia and the Far East, to name only a few, and in general to make her a participant in observing a common code of international behavior. But we have consistently tried to block admission of Communist China to the U.N., with gradually lessening majorities as more and more new nations add their votes in the General Assembly. One obvious result of this situation is that the good offices of the U.N. cannot easily be brought to bear in resolving conflicts like that in Vietnam.

When we look for an explanation of this self-defeating impasse, we find Nationalist China sitting like a sacred cow right smack in the pathway of rational policy. Actually, it was a pre-civil war, united China that was a signatory to the U.N. Charter in January, 1942, at San Francisco; therefore, legalistically, the question is not the seating of a new member but a change in the government representing an old member. Since the Chinese civil war, a representative of the Nationalist regime on Taiwan has sat among the "Big Five" permanent members of the Security Council. To perceive how ridiculous this is, all one need do is look at a map of Asia, with little Taiwan sitting off the coast of mammoth mainland China—it would be only slightly more ridiculous to set Chiang Kai-shek and his government afloat on a U.S. battleship for twenty years and persist in calling *this* the legitimate government of all China! But, ridiculous or not, the dilemma remains: we cannot abandon the two million Chinese (and ten million Taiwanese) on Taiwan after so many years of support; yet we cannot have a rational foreign policy without according Communist China, with one-fourth the population of the earth, its legitimate status within the U.N. It is also obvious that, given our long resistance to China's admission and our present level of hostility, we cannot directly and abruptly change our tune and expect conciliatory behavior from China.

If, at the highest level, our government would accept the fundamental irrationality of its position with regard to China and the U.N., *then* certain steps could be taken, consistent with the long-term best interests of both Taiwan and ourselves. First, we could quietly encourage other countries to vote for admission of Communist China, while assuring Nationalist China of our support for its independence unless and until it can work out some resolution with the mainland. Second, we could pave the way for eventual substitution of mainland China for Taiwan on the Security Council (a) by publicly announcing that we were enforcing an end to military threats and excursions from Taiwan against the mainland, as well as demilitarizing the off-shore islands of Quemoy and Matsu, and (b) by publicly announcing that we do not consider the Nationalist regime on Taiwan to be the legitimate government of all China. (Note that this last does *not* state that the Communist government in Peking *is* the legitimate government of all China, including Taiwan, but rather leaves this complex matter open to continuing discussions.)

Apart from their long-term rationality, there are several advantages to such steps as these. From a politico-military viewpoint, demilitarizing the off-shore islands and restraining Nationalist excursions against the mainland would remove one of the most continuous sources of irritation for the mainland Chinese; however, in keeping with GRIT strategy, it would have to be made clear that any attempt by the Communists to take over these islands aggressively would be met with firm resistance by the U.S. itself. From a psychological point of view, it can be predicted that public statements about restraining Chiang Kai-shek and about his government not being the legitimate one for all China would create severe cognitive stress in the world view of the mainland Chinese. In the simple-minded workings of psycho-logic, it is consistent and proper for those you dislike (the U.S. and Chiang Kai-shek in the view of the Communist Chinese) to agree with and support each other and to be against you; it is inconsistent, and downright disturbing, for those you dislike to disagree with each other. Witness the difficulty our State Department had in accepting the Sino-Soviet split. If such a situation is prolonged or repeated over time, something usually gives, and in this case it would probably be the implacably negative attitude toward the United States, since we would be behaving positively with respect to mainland China's goals.

But what about our relations with the Nationalist government on Taiwan? Great stress would be created there as well, and it could result simultaneously in less positive attitudes toward the U.S. and (paradoxically) less negative attitudes toward the Communist government on the mainland. To the extent that there were angry verbal exchanges—armed conflict between Taiwan and the U.S. seems most unlikely—this would simply heighten the predicted effects on all sides. If this seems like using a friend to placate an enemy, may I say that this is precisely what is often necessary for the long-term good of all concerned—and the enemies of today may become the friends of tomorrow. From the point of view of the

Taiwanese, they should realize that they would be the first to go, should a full-scale war develop between the United States and Communist China. They should also be continually assured that we will support their security and independence, until such time as they themselves work out a satisfactory arrangement with mainland China. In any case, we cannot remain hamstrung by this dilemma indefinitely, and our own long-term security depends far more upon a rapprochement with mainland China than upon our relations with Taiwan.

FANTASY OR NECESSITY?

To some readers the substance of this chapter may have seemed like pure fantasy, entirely removed from the hard facts of the real world. To the contrary, I submit that some kind of calculated de-escalation of the sort I have suggested, although certainly differing in details, is a necessity if we are to avoid the equally unpalatable alternatives of an immoral preventive war now or an unimaginably devastating nuclear war later. What makes even calculated de-escalation of tensions with China seem like fantasy to some Americans? I think it comes down to another unquestioned assumption: that the primary motivation of Chinese policy toward the United States is *aggression.* Let me suggest a different interpretation: that the admittedly belligerent verbal behavior of the Chinese toward this country is based primarily on *fear.* Militarily, China is weak as compared with the United States, if one computes on the basis of the entire arsenal, including nuclear capabilities. Assuming the same inherent aggressiveness in us that we assume in them, the Chinese growl and threaten in the hope of scaring us off—but they are extraordinarily cautious about what they actually do. If the primary motive *is* fear of us, as was the case with the Russians, then calculated de-escalation tactics have a good chance of succeeding.

There are other bases for optimism about such a course. For one thing, the old, hard-line revolutionaries like Mao, who have held tight control in China, are nearing Nature's retirement age; perhaps, as was the case in the Soviet Union, the younger men who assume control will be a bit more susceptible to reason. Both Chinese and Americans have strong motives of *self-interest* to avoid all-out conflict. If I am right, then application of GRIT can be begun on the basis of self-interest and, given the psychological effects of reciprocating, can itself create increasing mutual understanding and trust. Another basis, as I mentioned earlier, is the basic harmony between American and Chinese modes of interpersonal behavior. It is a common observation (which I share on the basis of my own cross-cultural reasearch experiences) that the Chinese tend to be outgoing, openly expressive of feelings, and by nature rather informal in their relations with others—like most Americans. It seems unlikely that even twenty years under a communist system will have eliminated such deep-seated traits. Reciprocal trade, communications, and tourism could revive good relations.

But we will never know the answers to these questions unless we have the courage and patience to find them out. As long as we keep on escalating militarily in Vietnam, we are not going to be able to find out how China would, in fact, react to a persistent policy of de-escalation. I have stressed our relation with Communist China because I see this as the crux of our future foreign policy problems. But our involvement in Vietnam has us handcuffed as far as effectively initiating a long-term policy toward Asia. Therefore we must ask what can be done now to damp the conflict in Vietnam.

CHAPTER 5

But What Do We Do in Vietnam?

I RECALL with wry pleasure a long after-hours discussion with John McNaughton, now Assistant Secretary of Defense for International Security Affairs, at a conference on Communications and Public Policy in 1961. I was defending the strategy of GRIT, and every so often he would punctuate my exposition with this question: "But what do we do in Berlin?" I realized then, as I realize now, that it is not easy to bring abstract policy to bear upon specific real-world situations. But this does not mean that debate over policy alternatives is fruitless nor that long-term policy cannot be related to day-to-day decisions. It just means that it is not easy, and I sympathize with, rather than envy, our people in critical decision-making positions. What follows is an attempt to relate the policy framework I have been developing to the specific situation in Vietnam.

THE LEDGER ON VIETNAM

Vietnam is one of the more recent instances of successful rebellion against European Colonialism. Through the early 1950's, France fought a grim, losing battle against the variety of nationalism represented by Ho Chi Minh. The 1954 Geneva agreement provided for a *temporary* division of Vietnam into North and South, with free elections to be held in 1956, and allowed the French to pull out of an impossible situation; it allowed the U.S., which had been supporting the French, to get into an impossible situation. We refused to allow free elections in 1956, because it was obvious (a) that they would not be free in the North and (b) that they would go 80 per cent or more for Ho Chi Minh, popular symbol of national unification, in the South. The rebellion of the Viet Cong against the government of Diem began soon after the failure to hold elections—but far to the south, not along the border with North Vietnam.

Our Commitment in Vietnam

Just precisely what is our "commitment" in South Vietnam? Here I return to the analysis given by Don and Arthur Larson in *Vietnam and Beyond,* the former being a political scientist and specialist in Asian affairs and the latter being a lawyer specializing in international relations. First, the United States was not a signatory to the Geneva agreement of 1954—and, in any case, this agreement has been broken repeatedly by both sides. Second, a letter from President Eisenhower to the then President Diem of South Vietnam in 1954 (which has been cited as a kind of commitment) merely states that our ambassador is instructed to "examine" a program of American aid and ends with the "hope" that needed reforms will be undertaken to be "responsive to the nationalist aspirations of its people." The third document cited is the SEATO Treaty, ratified in February, 1955: The relevant portion states that when "the territory or the sovereignty or political independence of any (covered area) . . . is threatened by any fact or situation which might endanger the peace of the area . . . *the parties shall consult immediately in order to agree on the measures which should be taken for the common defense*" (italics mine). There have been consultations but no agreements on measures—our actions have been unilateral.

Perhaps the simplest—if not the most eloquent—statement of our *lack* of commitment is to be found in an interview with President Kennedy by CBS newsman Walter Cronkite, in September, 1963, shortly before the assassination. President Kennedy said: "I don't think that unless a greater effort is made by the Government to win popular support that the war can be won out there. In the final analysis, it is their war. They are the ones who have to win it or lose it . . . and, in my opinion, in the last two months the Government has gotten out of touch with the people." As of this writing, the government of South Vietnam is once again getting out of touch with the people; Buddhists and students are on the march against the government of General Ky, and what is most significant to observe is the fact that resentment against U.S. "control" in South Vietnam is being openly expressed.

As a matter of fact, we did not hear much about our commitment in Vietnam until after President Johnson won his own election in a landslide against Barry Goldwater and was inaugurated. Statements about our commitment paralleled the military escalation of the war, as did statements about our actions being in response to "aggression from the North." Both sets of statements were hotly debated by academics across the country. The evidence then for armed invasion of South Vietnam by North Vietnam was very flimsy, as a careful reading of the State Department's "White Paper" on Vietnam (February, 1965) indicates. It was difficult to definitely identify as many as ten captured guerrillas who had been born and raised in the North. The fact that there are now North Vietnamese regulars fighting in the South cannot justify our escalation in February of 1965. The truth of the matter seems to be that we had no legal or binding commitment in Vietnam. Rather, we have *created* the sense of commitment—and it is really to ourselves, to resist militarily any shift to any form of Communism anywhere on the globe.

Potential Gains of Our Present Policy

We must be realistic about potential political gains and losses in Vietnam. What might we stand to gain? Under the most favorable circumstances imaginable for us, the North Vietnamese would agree to negotiate from a position of weakness, before the Chinese became involved overtly and before we cross the "Nuclear war is unthinkable" threshold.

The Administration has stated repeatedly that the purpose of the military escalation in Vietnam is to force our opponents to the negotation table. I have already discussed the irrationality of this attempt to mix escalation and de-escalation strategies. During the month-long lull in our bombing of North Vietnam, the President sent off a flurry of diplomatic doves in what was called, rather militantly, a great "Peace Offensive." According to Secretary Rusk (AP, January 21, 1966), this peace offensive was highly successful in winning the approval of many countries for our policies—but it was an abject failure in its avowed purpose of getting people to the conference table. Asked whether the war might now spread into other areas, Rusk said: "There is always danger when an aggressor sets out to impose his will by force and the other side is determined to keep its commitments." Would that we had the gift to see ourselves as others see us!

Another potential gain that has been repeatedly stated is the right of the people of South Vietnam to "self-determination." Sadly enough, as used in the context of Vietnam, this is another bit of our own tired semantics—much sound and little substance. Can it be denied that the Viet Cong, and the Viet Minh before them against the French, have been fighting for "self-determination" as they happen to view it? Are we so naïve as to believe that any negotiated settlement would end the attempts of these people to "liberate" South Vietnam? The dictatorships we have supported there certainly have little support from the people. After such a settlement, would we agree to hold free elections—when some 70 per cent of the country is still under Viet Cong control? We were not willing to risk even the shadow of the possibility of Communism in the Dominican Republic, and I doubt very much if we would respond differently in Vietnam. I have visions of a cartoon Bill Mauldin might draw: a giant leatherneck stands with one booted foot on a devastated North Vietnam and the other on an equally devastated South Vietnam, and he is saying, "Wal . . . we sure gave these little fellas the right to self-determination!"

Yet another potential gain often mentioned is that our demonstration of military strength and determination in Vietnam will convince the Communist Chinese that we are a real, not a paper, Tiger, thus damping their expansionist ambition. I am sure the Chinese leadership has not the slightest doubt about the U.S. being a real military Tiger; indeed, everything in their behavior (if not their words) over the past decade has been a demonstration of this conviction. But what do the Chinese *do* when faced with a real and very threatening Tiger? Just what we would do under similar circumstances, I think—try to buy the time and build the weapons needed to fight a Real Tiger.

Undoubtedly the deepest concern we have in Vietnam stems from the "domino theory," which in turn goes back to our continuing policy of containment of world Communism. Our leadership perceives the Viet Cong rebellion, directed from Hanoi and inspired in Peking, as the testing ground of a new communist strategy for achieving world domination even within the limitations imposed by the nuclear age. This new strategy is the so-called "war of national liberation." The domino argument is that if this strategy is allowed to succeed in South Vietnam, and it goes communist, then it will be applied in Cambodia, then Laos, then Thailand, then India, and eventually exported to Africa, South America, and everywhere across the globe.

The issue, of course, is whether the major pressure toward "liberation" is indigenous to a country (in which case it is a legitimate rebellion and that country's own concern) or the major pressure comes from outside (in which case it constitutes illegitimate subversion or invasion and may be our concern). Given the determined and successful rebellion against the French and the obvious unpopularity of subsequent puppet governments of South Vietnam, I think we must conclude that the Viet Cong rebellion against Diem was, in fact, a legitimate attempt at liberation, supported but by no means contrived by Hanoi or Peking. If this is the case, then by first intervening in the South and then escalating against the North, *we* have transformed the conflict there into a test of global strategies—and the Vietnamese people are the certain losers.

In general, physical analogies like the "domino theory" should be handled with caution. They are slippery semantically. In the real world of human affairs "dominoes" can fall in ways that impede rather than speed the flow of a political philosophy. The Soviet Union has discovered this. And the real lesson of Munich, as Hitler discovered in his bomb shelter at the end of World War II, was that falling dominoes usually make others more, not less, resistant to pressure.

At the end of the line of potential gains from escalation in Vietnam there is the materially insignificant, but psychologically and politically most significant, matter of saving face. Many people will argue that we shouldn't be in Vietnam at all, but now that we are there through a long series of mistakes, and our boys are dying for them, we've got to force our opponents to the negotiation table simply in order to be able to withdraw gracefully. All I can say to this is that if we have nothing more to gain from negotiations than face-saving, then we have decided to wage a dirty and dangerous war—with not only American lives but hundreds of thousands of Vietnamese lives as well being sacrificed—in order to win a political defeat that could be achieved much more easily and honorably otherwise. As to the matter of saving face, it would be wise for Americans to keep in mind that France not only withdrew from Vietnam but also later from Algeria; I find it hard to discern today the slightest loss of face for de Gaulle or for France because of these withdrawals.

Potential Losses from Our Present Policy

What do we stand to *lose* by continuing our present policies in Vietnam? These losses can be summarized very succinctly—because they are already operating and in evidence. We are alienating neutrals like India and taxing

the capacities of allies like Canada and Japan to rationalize
our actions. We have undercut the authority and prestige of
the U.N., just as seriously as did the Russians by refusing to
pay their share of the peace-keeping operations in the Congo.
We have lost the momentum gained over the past few years
in calculated de-escalation vis-à-vis the Soviet Union, and
we have greatly restricted the possibilities of applying this
strategy to China. In the eyes of much of the world, we have
catapulted the Soviets into the role of moderate peace-seeker
between two intolerant extremists—leftist China and rightist
America. Witness Russia's recent role in easing the conflict
between India and Pakistan. We are wallowing into a jungle
land war in Asia that we have been well advised by past
leaders to avoid at all cost.

Most important, I think, by employing a strategy that is
fundamentally inappropriate in a nuclear age, we have made
it easier to continue on this course and much more difficult
to return to one that is appropriate in the long run. A national
image of patience, firmness, reasonableness, and dependa-
bility is easy to destroy but difficult to build. We are likely
to remain glued to the escalator and continue at an accelerating pace toward a Pax Americana that ill fits both our ideals
and our capabilities. The Chinese, still living in terms of
their own past experiences, are likely to help us in the escalation process. This is not a pretty picture of the future.

Negotiated Settlement as the Goal of Present Policy

The stated purpose of the military escalation in Vietnam
is to force our opponents to the negotiation table. This *goal*
has been accepted without question, by supporters and
critics of government strategy alike. But, like everything else
in this complicated situation, even this apparently reasonable
and moral goal requires careful inspection. Let us suppose
that, somehow, we and our opponents do arrive at the
negotiating table: *precisely what would we be negotiating
for?* Aside from some rather vague statements about preserv-
ing the right to self-determination for the South Vietnamese,

very little has been said publicly about this important matter. Do we have a well thought out and reasonable bargaining position? Or is it the case that we haven't the foggiest notion of what is and is not negotiable—and hence that this goal is an illusion? In the absence of official guidance, we must speculate for ourselves.

Would we negotiate for a Vietnam permanently divided into Communist North and Democratic South? Not only would such permanent division be contrary to the expressed intent of the Geneva Accord of 1954, but it seems certain that this division could only be maintained by continuing U.S. military presence in South Vietnam. Certainly the Communists are not going to accept a solution which requires them to withdraw militarily and allows us to remain—unless the negotiations are in fact terms of surrender. Indeed, could we expect the North Vietnamese and Viet Cong to honor the terms of any agreement which they had been bombed into signing? It seems clear that such an arbitrary dividing line between two halves of what the Vietnamese people believe to be a single country—with antagonistic political philosophies trying to operate on the two sides— would be a constant source of friction and conflict.

Would we negotiate for a reunified and neutralized Vietnam? This would involve withdrawal of the military forces of both North Vietnam and the United States (presumably with substitution of U.N. peace-keeping forces), guarantees of the political integrity of existing governments in both North and South Vietnam, and agreements to respect the integrity of a reunified Vietnam, regardless of its political complexion. Unification might be arrived at either by free and supervised elections or by arrangements between the governments of North and South. But, in either case, it seems a certainty that any unified government would be some type of Communism; the North is uniformly Communist and some 70 per cent of the South is under Viet Cong control. Nevertheless, given the traditional resistance of the Vietnamese to Chinese domination, such a unified government should be relatively neutral and also reasonably stable. In other words, a reunified Vietnam could have the effect of "containing" the expansion of Chinese domination in Asia, regardless of its own political character.

But here we come to the nub of the whole matter. *Is the United States prepared to accept any solution which would mean a communist government in South Vietnam?* Do we accept the principle of self-determination if what the people determine for themselves is a form of Communism? If I read the mood of this country correctly, it is not prepared to accept any such solution. We have built one of our dikes against Communism in Vietnam—albeit on shaky ground—and we appear determined to hold it at any cost. It is becoming clearer and clearer in the public statements of our leaders that we are making this a part of *our* war against Communism—particularly of the Chinese variety. I am going to use some harsh words, but I believe the situation warrants them: it would appear that *we* have decided that the Vietnamese people are better Dead than Red.

The issue of *principle* ought to be whether or not the Vietnamese people want us there and are in any sense ready to assume a democratic way of life. The repeated claim—that Diem and the governments after his in kaleidoscopic array have "invited" us to stay and to keep increasing our military involvement—is a transparent rationalization. These governments are our puppets and they certainly have been neither democratic nor representative of the people. If we get the impression that most of the people want us there, it is largely because we talk mainly to those most Westernized (Catholic) Vietnamese whose positions depend on our presence, because the South Vietnamese peasants in areas we control are afraid to speak frankly, and because we do not talk at all to the Viet Cong or their political representatives, the National Liberation Front. I think a more accurate picture would be that, in the eyes of most Vietnamese, we are the colonial French all over again, even if in somewhat different garb and making somewhat different noises. Behind our

backs, they call us "the big-nosed white faces." After twenty
years of war on their soil, what these people want above all
is peace and a chance to rebuild their shattered lives.

It may well be that my vision is not as clear as it might be,
but I am unable to imagine *any* negotiated settlement that
would simultaneously guarantee an independent, non-communist South Vietnam and permit the withdrawal and
return home of our own military forces. If this is the case,
then the Administration should tell us so and cease using the
hope of a negotiated settlement as the excuse for all this
ugliness. If we construe the conflict in Vietnam as essentially
military, then even prudent, gradual withdrawal would
obviously be a defeat. If we view this conflict as essentially
political, however, then withdrawal can be considered a strategic retreat—in an area where we had practically no hope
of a political victory to begin with. The consequences of
continued escalation remain incalculably more dangerous
than the consequences of prudent withdrawal. If this is not
the case—and we do have something to gain from a negotiated settlement—then the Administration should let us know
precisely what we would be negotiating for.

ALTERNATIVES IN VIETNAM

Let me say immediately that I do not believe that there
is any *attractive* alternative for us in Vietnam at this point.
We have gotten ourselves into a politically and morally in-
defensible position there by following the ghostly finger of
John Foster Dulles to the inevitable conclusion of his policy
of containment of Communism. In order to implement this
policy in a place where it was obviously failing, we swallowed the baited hook of military escalation. It will be painful to tear ourselves off, but to remain hooked means suicide,
if not for our lives then certainly for our way of life. The
longer we stay hooked, the longer we are prevented from
effectively applying rational policies elsewhere as well.

Those who speak glibly of "victory" either have no conception of what a prolonged land war in Southeast Asia would be like (if we keep it that way), or have no conception of what genocide does to those who practice it (if we escalate into the nuclear range), or are selfishly and short-sightedly trying to feather their own political nests at the expense of the ordinary people in this world. On the other hand, those who keep demanding U.S. withdrawal from Vietnam—abjectly and unconditionally—either have no conception of the state of the public mind and the pressures upon our leadership, or are trying to guarantee a place for themselves in Heaven at the expense of the well-being of ordinary people in the here and now. I believe there is a viable alternative that lies between these extremes, but it is only attractive in comparison and is certainly not an easy way out.

First, there is a fundamental decision which can only be made at the very top of our decision-making hierarchy, by President Lyndon Johnson himself. *This is to shift absolutely from an escalation strategy to a de-escalation strategy.* The kind of de-escalation strategy embodied in GRIT includes firm resistance to aggressive attempts by an opponent to change the status quo, but it also includes the persistent application of initiatives designed to decrease tensions and increase the prospects for non-violent resolution of conflict.

What does this mean with respect to Vietnam? Actually, President Johnson has laid the ground for just such an approach in some of his statements. He has made it clear that we cannot and will not be driven out of Vietnam by aggressive military means; he has also made it clear that we desire a non-violent solution. What remains is to implement this position, rather than use it as a justification for an entirely different strategy. Here is what I think would be involved in implementing calculated de-escalation of the conflict in Vietnam:

(1) *We announce exactly the extent of the present status quo and our intention to maintain it against any aggressive attempts at change.* This could take the form of "enclaves" of control, as suggested by Senator Fulbright, or it could

take the form of maintaining constant resistance to infiltration of men or supplies from the north, while maintaining the existing regions of our control within South Vietnam. Having announced this intent, we stick to it with everything we've got—even though we might save more of our own men in the short run by escalating. The essential thing is to create a stalemate sufficiently prolonged to allow us to apply intense pressures toward other solutions.

(2) *We gradually pull back the radius of our bombing of North Vietnam.* This would be either to the border between North and South Vietnam, or to the perimeters of our enclaves, depending upon the option taken under (1) above. This would decrease the likelihood of Chinese involvement, give the North Vietnamese bona fide evidence that we mean what we say, and remove the major obstacle for the Russians in serving as mediators with the North Vietnamese.

(3) *We announce that we are prepared to negotiate unconditionally with all parties concerned.* "All parties" must include political representatives of the Viet Cong (the National Liberation Front), on their own rather than as part of any North Vietnamese delegation—the latter being equivalent to asking them to accept our definition of the war as being directed from Hanoi. This should be made explicit. We cannot expect our opponents to leap at this opportunity when it is first offered. However, we are powerful enough to maintain our firmness under the conditions of (1) while waiting for the wisdom of a non-violent solution to sink in.

In the meantime, if we really want to get out of Southeast Asia with dignity and in the foreseeable future, we can support a gradual broadening of the democratic base of the Saigon government, first, by encouraging the Buddhists and Catholics to bridge their gulf and participate in a common government, and second, by encouraging political leaders of the Viet Cong to become involved in the government, thereby making it more representative. Tran Van Huu, a former Vietnamese prime minister (writing in *War/Peace Report*, November, 1965) points out that "Right now, ... there is no communication between the Liberation Front and the Americans. But some link must be created for two reasons: first, to give the Liberation Front leadership a more worthwhile opposite number to deal with than the discredited generals, and second, to bring the Americans to accept a political solution." We cannot force an alienated puppet government down the throats of a Vietnamese people who have been fighting for "self-determination" for nearly twenty years.

(4) *We undertake a pattern of displaced initiatives* (such as I have described earlier) *designed to damp tensions and change our world image.* This is done across the global board, while we are standing firm under the conditions of (1) above. Is such a posture—simultaneously maintaining firm military resistance at the focus of conflict while supporting a set of deliberate tension-reducing moves elsewhere—unrealistic? No. It is obviously possible for rational governments to behave this way; it is merely contrary to tradition and emotion.

Given these underlying conditions, one can imagine several possible developments. (a) There could be a gradual de-escalation of the intensity of the conflict, with South Vietnamese soldiers drifting back into their villages and their ordinary lives and both North Vietnamese and American soldiers being brought back to their homelands in increasing numbers—a kind of de facto end to hostilities. This would increase the prospects for shifting the problem into the hands of the U.N. (b) There could be gradual changes in the complexion of the Saigon government (with our tacit support) to the point where it would be prepared to deal directly with North Vietnam on the matter of unification— and we would be asked politely to terminate our military presence but continue our economic and social support. By that time, I am sure the United States would be entirely happy to do just this. (c) After some period of getting used to the new look of things, the North Vietnamese and Viet Cong (with the encouragement of the Soviet Union and perhaps even of China, if we have played our de-escalation cards well) would indicate their readiness to sit down at the negotiation table and talk. And what should we bargain for? I think we should go right back to the Geneva Accord, with its provisions for subsequent elections toward a unified Vietnam; we should also insist on guarantees against reprisals and fair representation in any government of the Catholic minority, and we should try to obtain guarantees of the integrity of neighboring countries like Thailand.

We have great power for either good or evil in this world. We also have our own long-term survival to insure. The kind of calculated de-escalation I have proposed here has been rendered much more difficult by the military escalation that has already taken place, and each new step in escalation will increase the difficulty even further. We are, indeed, in the position of the losing gambler who thinks that by merely increasing the size of his bets he can come out winning. What is needed is a completely new strategy. We have gotten ourselves into an incredible mess in Vietnam, and it is going to take an equally incredible effort at reason to get us out.

SOME LESSONS TO BE LEARNED FROM VIETNAM

Regardless of how long it takes us to get disentangled in Southeast Asia, there are some important lessons to be learned from the crisis in Vietnam as well as from other crises in our recent history, like those in Cuba and the Dominican Republic. I believe that nations, just like individuals, survive and are successful to the extent that they learn the right lessons from their experiences. The Russians learned something important about survival in a nuclear age from the Cuban missile crisis; they learned the right lesson—"you don't try to change the status quo with respect to another major power by escalating aggressively in his own backyard" —but we obviously did not. From among the many lessons to be learned from Vietnam, I select only the following, which I consider the most salient.

Lesson I: that our assumption of a monolithic, unmodifiable, and implacably hostile world Communism creates a self-fulfilling but self-defeating prophecy.

By defining the rebellion of the Viet Cong as being directed from Hanoi and inspired by Peking, and by then escalating militarily against this so-defined external aggression, we have increased both the dependence of the Viet Cong upon the North Vietnamese and, in turn, the dependence of North Vietnam upon the Communist Chinese. In other words, where there has been considerable independence of the Viet Cong from the direction and control of Hanoi, and certainly of Hanoi from the control of Peking, we are busily creating the very communist monolith in Asia we have assumed to exist. This is self-defeating. Similarly, by assuming communist control over the revolution in the Dominican Republic, and by taking military actions consistent with this assumption, we have probably done more to increase communist influence in Latin America than Castro has been able to do in several years. This is self-defeating.

Lesson II: that by projecting our own world view upon others and not trying to perceive issues as they see them, our benevolence is misconstrued, our power is misspent, and our world leadership becomes inept.

The most fundamental issue in today's world is the inequity between "have" and "have-not" countries and between "have" and "have-not" peoples within countries. By misperceiving this fundamental issue as being a quasi-religious conflict between world Communism and a so-called Free World, we repeatedly identify the "haves" as being on our side and the "have-nots" as being on the side of the opposition. Thus our foreign aid is more military than economic, and it is actually used to exaggerate rather than reduce existing inequities in the status quo. By widening the gulf between the rural peasantries and the urban aris-

tocracies we support (because they are the most Westernized, the most wealthy, and hence most anti-communist),
we are sowing the seeds for prolonged and intensified rebellion and revolution. This, too, is self-defeating.

*Lesson III: that the use of military escalation as a political
tool blocks all other approaches to world problems and is
incompatible with our long-term goals.*

This is a very difficult lesson for a powerful nation to learn.
As long as unused reserves of military power remain, there
is great temptation to use them, once the psychological dynamics of conflict are fully operative. Yet the course of history is strewn with the relics of nations which failed to learn
that Might does not necessarily make Right. If "getting our
way" is defined as anything other than simply eliminating
anyone who disagrees with us, then it is clear that the application of raw military power has its limitations as a means
of persuasion. Buddhists and students in the cities of South
Vietnam are now marching the streets chanting "Americans
go home!" To be sure, we have the power to stay there
whether they want us or not; indeed, we have the power to
wipe both North and South Vietnam clean of all life and
vegetation. We might even be able to convince ourselves
that all this was necessary—"to contain Communism." But
we would have learned the wrong lesson and would be
headed toward an ugly future, with America as the ugliest
part of it. The time may be near when even our friends in
Vietnam will be begging us to leave them alone, to go away
and take all of our terrible and terrifying war machines with
us. I only hope that our leadership will have the foresight and
humanity to make the right decision.

*Lesson IV: that our semantic maps of the real world are
becoming outmoded at an increasingly rapid rate and need
radical revision if we are to survive with the technology we
have created.*

What this species needs, and that most desperately, is a
full-scale revolution in its semantics. As one moves outward
from the intimate family toward the community, the nation,
and the world, the misfit of word to thing becomes greater

and greater. While developments in technology—in transportation, in communication, in automation, in computerization, to say nothing of weaponry—are moving at a constantly accelerating pace and are rapidly shrinking this globe, our semantic maps of it are changing at the pace of a reluctant, suction-footed snail. Rather than trying to adapt our meanings of words to the changing nature of the things they refer to, we persist in trying to force things to conform to the antiquated meanings our words already have, and we behave more and more like Alices in Wonderlands because of this.

We need a healthy suspicion of the implications of familiar words and phrases. Take for example the notion of "mutual security pacts." We have such pacts all over the globe— NATO is one of them, SEATO is another. The phrase certainly *sounds* pretty good, but not a single word in it means anything like what it seems to mean when fitted to the real world. They are not at all "mutual"; rather they are obviously dominated by the U.S. and aimed at the containment of Communism. They have little to do with "security" in a nuclear age—certainly not for the U.S. and probably not for the other countries involved. They are "pacts" only as long as they are consistent with self-interest; de Gaulle's France is now pulling out of NATO and moving toward the Soviet Union, for what it now perceives as its self-interest. Our Administration's spokesmen are fond of talking about "democratic" South Vietnam and about "self-determination" for its people; but there never has been anything democratic about the governments of South Vietnam, and we have already seen how poorly the notion of self-determination fits the reality of our presence there. The so-called "Free World" is as sorry and jumbled a set of ill-assorted types of governments as one could find, and more of them are being taken over by military dictatorships every year. I have heard officers in our own military say quite openly that they prefer to deal with military governments—"they talk our language, we can do business with them"; at least, these men are not misusing terms.

We need an imaginative flexibility in the development of

new language and the use of old. Old semantics binds our thinking; fresh semantics can help to free it. "When I use a word," Humpty Dumpty said, in rather a scornful tone, "it means just what I choose it to mean, neither more nor less." "The question is," said Alice, "whether you *can* make words mean so many different things." "The question is," said Humpty Dumpty, "which is to be master, that's all." The English language is full of linguistic means for framing new concepts. A nub that can be attached to a sperl in order to make it synchronize with an unbalanced loober may come to be called *an unbalanced loober sperl-nub synchronizer* —and, if used frequently enough, *a loob-synch.* But the problem, of course, is to fit the implications of the name to the real-world properties of the thing. Wouldn't we be in a terrible fix if, in fact, sperl-nubs could only synchronize with *balanced* loobers! Our news media only too easily slide from "rebels" to "Communists" to "Reds" in any conflict situation; "Viet Cong" and the more handy and dashing (for headline purposes) "Reds" have become completely interchangeable now. Yet the Viet Cong are by no means all Communists, and, as a matter of fact, only a relatively small proportion of them were at the point of our escalation in Vietnam. How we behave in Vietnam—in the conduct of the war, in our conception of the Saigon government, in our position on negotiations—depends upon the precision with which we talk about things.

We need more respect for the distinction between words and things. A State Department expert on Asian affairs and I have been carrying on a lengthy—and only occasionally acrimonious—debate by correspondence. In one letter he says, "I submit that you simply cannot read the public statements made by Chinese Communist . . . leaders and articles in their controlled press without having an unmistakable impression of implacable hostility." Fair enough: Chinese public statements rattle like the bones of a skeleton with tired, dusty phrases—"imperialist warmongers," "the criminals in the Pentagon and Wall Street," and so on *ad nauseam.*

But I am sure that this State Department official's opposite number in Peking can easily find statements by leaders in this country displaying equally implacable hostility and filled with equally tired and dusty ideological symbols.

I am also reminded of the furor caused by Khrushchev's offhand statement, "We will bury you!"—which, as I understand it, was an unfortunately literal translation of a Russian idiom meaning something like "we'll leave you in the dust by winning the competition." The point is that this statement, along with all the ideological jargon of both the Russians and the Chinese, is being used as *proof* of communist intentions in the real world. We would be wise to pay less attention to what is said on both sides and more attention to what is done. Their semantic maps are certainly no better than our own, and, given their greater control over public dissent, probably much worse.

In concluding this chapter, I can do no better than offer you a quotation from one of the geniuses of our century, Albert Einstein. Writing as a physical scientist and mathematician many years ago, and displaying the real breadth of perspective we associate with true genius, he had this to say: "Our world is threatened by a crisis whose extent seems to escape those within whose power it is to make major decisions for good or evil. The unleashed power of the atom has changed everything except our ways of thinking. Thus we are drifting toward a catastrophe beyond comparison. We shall require a substantially new manner of thinking if mankind is to survive."

Epilogue: Patience

Rome wasn't built in a day and neither will be security for a free world. As participants in a young and bustling society, most Americans are impatient, and I think our President well represents us in this matter. We are also terribly insecure about ourselves and our own values. But, impatient and often unloved, we are nevertheless the most powerful nation on the face of the earth. It is time we grew up enough *inside* to be able to meet our responsibilities *outside*. Mature nations, like mature people, must come to take the long view in both space and time.

Like the Cuban missile crisis and like the situation in the Dominican Republic, Vietnam is a learning experience. It is only one trial among many that have preceded and many that will follow. But how we behave as a nation in this trial will have its effect upon how we behave in the future. The danger is that we will be learning that Might makes Right, learning to use our military power in an attempt to make the world over in our own image. The truth is that we are by no means a good enough image, we do not have enough power to accomplish such a goal, even if it were worthy, and we will certainly change ourselves more than we change others in the process. The hope is that we will learn some valuable lessons from this experience, lessons that will enable us to be more sensitive, more flexible, and more sensible in future crises. But to the extent that we are successful, moving toward a more secure world will be a very long process, and it will require a great deal of *patience*.

We cannot expect peoples everywhere to make the "great

leap forward" into democracy the moment they obtain self-government and freedom from internal and external oppression. Democracy, as found in these United States, for example, is a complex web of traditions, practices, values, and expectations. The fundamental notion of civil rights—which we are *still* struggling to establish after nearly 200 years of democracy—cannot be donned like a new hat by the people in Indonesia, let us say, who have had no preparation. The practice of free election becomes a travesty in a country where few can read or write and most do not even know they are citizens of a nation. As Don and Arthur Larson put it (in *Vietnam and Beyond*), ". . . with a very few exceptions, the fragile new "democracies" have one by one given way to some species of strong man rule, sometimes beneficent, sometimes not. In retrospect it seems inconceivable that anyone could have expected democracy in a country like the Congo, which had 18 college graduates and 21 political parties on its Independence Day."

To a book that is already prickly with heresy, let me add yet another spine. I believe it may be necessary for under-powered countries to go through some form of totalitarianism, be it dictatorship or Communism, in order to create even the minimum conditions for a democratic way of life. These minimum conditions include freedom from perpetual hunger, freedom from perpetual ignorance, and freedom from perpetual fear. Some of the strong-man governments which we support have tried to create these minimum freedoms, while others have not; but so also have some communist governments tried to bring these minimum freedoms to their people. In under-powered countries it is often necessary to literally compel many people to forgo immediate gratifications—they have so little to enjoy—in order to build the capital upon which a spiral of economic development can be begun. *Some* ideology that sets hope on the future—be it religious, nationalistic, communistic, or all of these at once—is required. If we have the patience to take a "moon's-eye view" of our little planet and its struggles, we may be able to see Communism as a stage through which some regions must pass, given their existing conditions.

If this be the case, and I think it is, then the best way for a powerful nation like the United States to win the real war with Communism as a way of life is to help people move through and out of this stage as rapidly as possible. This means helping to create *in communist countries* those additional conditions which make their political system first awkward, then irritating, and eventually intolerable: economic conditions of well-being, which yield possessions individuals are reluctant to lose and also confer the sense of individuality; educational conditions of awareness and sensitivity, which yield opinions to express and new ideas to compete with old; international conditions of security, which yield no excuse for tyranny to withhold or withdraw individual freedoms.

Many people will argue that "once a country goes Communist, it stays Communist." Why? Because this type of government clamps the lid on freedom of thought as well as of speech and action. They will point to the fact that no country which has gone Communist has yet come out of it. My answer to this would be, first, that we have had very little time as cultures go, to observe change—Communism began with the revolution in Russia a scant fifty years ago—and second, that the existing communist societies have indeed been changing. It is a well-attested fact that individual freedoms have been increasing in the Soviet Union, along with increasing economic security, material well-being, and higher and higher levels of education; returning visitors report that the Russian people are jealous of these freedoms and would resist their withdrawal.

Along with these changes has come a decided decrease in the Soviet Union's belligerence—becoming a relatively "have" nation is one of the strongest inhibitors of aggression. Can we not expect similar changes to occur in China, given similar conditions? The fact that changes in expressed ideology occur more slowly should not disturb us; as anthropologists know, changes in real culture usually run far ahead of changes in ideal culture—and it is real culture that should be our concern.

But the kinds of changes in societies we are talking about take many generations. In the meantime, we need not only patience but a strategy for monitoring conflicts and rendering them amenable to non-lethal solutions. We need a strategy designed to gradually create the kind of atmosphere within which an orderly transfer from national to international sovereignty can occur. The nature of our present technology not only makes possible effective world government, it demands it if we are to survive much longer as a species.

The particular version of calculated de-escalation I have espoused in these pages—*graduated and reciprocated initiatives in tension-reduction* (or GRIT for short)—includes the features of firm resistance to attempts to change the status quo by military force (the stick) and techniques for inducing reciprocative tension-reducing steps from others (the carrot). Operating within reasonable limits of national security, GRIT applies the carrot and the stick persistently and predictably as a means of gaining gradual acceptance of a set of rules for international behavior that are appropriate to a nuclear age. But GRIT is not a glamorous policy. Its initiatives will never catch headlines the way a bombing attack on Hanoi would do. Indeed, it is a very slow and plodding process. Nevertheless, as Aesop taught us, the strategy of the Tortoise may be superior to the strategy of the Hare.

This kind of foreign policy is particularly feasible for a mature and powerful nation—if that nation has sufficient perspective and patience. The power we possess, both militarily and economically, makes it possible for us to take repeated initiatives of a calculated sort without jeopardizing our real security. Right now, our hands are tied by our involvement in Vietnam and we are unable to use our power effectively. The sooner we can ease the crisis there, the sooner we will be able to get down to the far more important job of working out a long-term relationship with the rest of the world. With the level of hostility reduced and communication barriers removed, there is much that we could do to "escalate" mutual trust and understanding. There is the matter of the Lower Mekong River Valley Development Project, recommended eight years ago by the United Nations Economic Commission for Asia. The lower Mekong affects the lives and fortunes of many millions of people, in Laos, Thailand, and Cambodia as well as in Vietnam. President Johnson has already expressed his willingness to seek one billion dollars to help the economies of countries in Southeast Asia. If we could enlist the help of the Soviets and even the Chinese, eventually, in such projects, so much the better.

Finally, let me express my sincere thanks to those members of the Senate and the House who have had the courage and statesmanship to raise the deep issues of our foreign policy to the level of open debate. I am sure that many, many other citizens of this country would join me in this expression of appreciation. It is the business of Congress to represent the people in affairs of government, and certainly the most important affair of government right now is the formulation of an enlightened long-term policy for our relations with the rest of this teeming, shrinking planet. Although it is, of course, true that the President cannot wait upon full-dress debate in Congress before making critical day-to-day decisions, Congress can make its legitimate influence felt by acting in anticipation of, rather than in response to, events in the world. Congress can help formulate a policy framework which puts the Vietnams of tomorrow into perspective and provides guidelines for the day-to-day actions of the Administration.